# YUMMY Discoveries
## — THE —
# Baby-Led Weaning Recipe Book

# YUMMY Discoveries
## —THE—
## Baby-Led Weaning Recipe Book

Felicity Bertin and Emma Ogden-Hooper

ROBERT HALE • LONDON

© Yummy Discoveries 2013
First published in Great Britain 2013

ISBN 978-0-7198-0698-8

Robert Hale Limited
Clerkenwell House
Clerkenwell Green
London EC1R 0HT

www.halebooks.com

The right of Felicity Bertin and Emma Ogden-Hooper to be identified as
authors of this work has been asserted by them
in accordance with the Copyright, Designs and
Patents Act 1988

The information in this book has been compiled by way of general guidance in relation to the specific
subjects addressed, but is not a substitute and not to be relied on for medical, healthcare,
pharmaceutical, or other professional advice. Parents and guardians are advised to consult their GP,
health visitor or other relevant healthcare professional if they are concerned about their child's health or
development and before changing, stopping or starting medical treatment. So far as the authors are
aware, the information given is accurate and up to date as of October 2012. Practice laws, regulation and
recommendations continuously change and the reader should obtain up-to-date professional advice on
any such issues. The authors and publishers disclaim, as far as the law allows, any liability arising
directly or indirectly from the use or misuse of the information contained in this book.

A catalogue record for this book is available from the British Library

2  4  6  8  10  9  7  5  3  1

Designed and illustrated by Eurodesign
Printed in China by 1010 Printing International Ltd

This book is dedicated
to our children, Lucas and Ethan,
who were our inspiration for producing it

# Acknowledgements

We would like to thank Gill Jackson at Robert Hale for giving us this opportunity and our editor Nikki Edwards for her constant patience in dealing with a couple of novice authors.

A big thank you goes to our friends and their families who willingly tested our recipes and shared their family favourites.

Felicity would like to thank her mum, Yvonne, for passing on her skills as a chef and for offering so much of her time and energy which enabled this book to be written.

Emma would like to give a special acknowledgement to her mum, Charlotte, whose home-cooked food instilled in Emma the desire to do the same for her family and whose recipes have contributed to this book.

Most importantly we would like to thank our husbands, Dave and Mark, for believing in us from the start, for reading (and re-reading!) the manuscript, and for all their love and support.

# Contents

# Message from Mummies

When I decided to wean Lucas, I got myself prepared with the food blender and ice cube trays, ready to purée the life out of every fruit and vegetable in my kitchen. Little did I know that my little one was going to shun the mush. I quickly had to change tack and started to research as much as I could about baby-led weaning. Unfortunately, there's not much information out there as the name of the game is 'your baby can eat everything you eat (with a few little do's and don'ts)'.

I thought I was a pretty good cook but when I opened my cupboards I found jars and packets laden with salt, sugar and other additives. I'd never made a bolognese or white sauce from scratch, instead choosing to fry some meat, adding a jar of whatever came to hand. With a 6-month-old resting on my hip, I didn't have time to mess around with long, complicated recipes and so began my journey of experimentation and producing healthy, tasty foods the whole family can enjoy.

These recipes are quick and easy, but most importantly they are healthy and suitable for both you and your child. The information in this book is honest about how long things take to make and their suitability for your freezer. We have tried to stick to foods that you can easily pick up in your local shop and repeatedly use the same ingredients to help reduce cost and waste. Some recipes will have further tips as to what you can do with any leftovers, helping your money go that little bit further.

I hope your family enjoy these recipes as much as mine do.

*Felicity*
X

PS. Throughout this book we've alternated the use of he and she to try to be fair to both girls and boys.

I always knew that the time would come when I would have to wean my son. Although I approached it with apprehension, fear and confusion, the one thing I knew for certain was that he would eat home-cooked food, and when the time finally arrived I decided to follow the more traditional method of weaning.

After the first few months of introducing puréed and mashed foods I noticed that my son became restless, bored and frustrated at mealtimes. However, I soon discovered that offering a variety of finger foods and allowing him to feed himself resulted in him enjoying mealtimes and he was once again happy to eat the mashed up foods alongside his finger foods.

The joy you get from watching your child enjoy your home-cooked food is second to none. While I can remember meals Ethan clearly disliked, (please do not get disheartened; it may take a couple of attempts for your child to eat certain foods) the numerous meals he has enjoyed have made up for it.

Cooking the recipes in this book has helped me introduce Ethan to different colours, textures and tastes, making mealtimes an exciting voyage of discovery for him.

Due to my experience of mealtimes with a toddler I strongly believe in the merits of allowing your child to feed themselves. Whether you are following baby-led weaning or a more traditional method, the independence of self-feeding plays a critical role by facilitating your child's development and their enjoyment of food. This recipe book, which has been written by parents for parents, will prove to be invaluable.

Emma x

# Navigating This Book

Throughout the recipes featured in this book you will see the following abbreviations or references:

✳ = Suitable for home freezing, see pages 218–19 for tips on freezing and defrosting

(P/LB) = Ideal foods for picnics or lunch boxes

(L/o) = Leftovers (as featured in the weekly meal planners on pages 17, 19 and 21)

*Tips* = Top tips from other parents to help make feeding your family easier

*Leftovers* = Suggestions as to what to do with any leftovers, which can help reduce waste, workload and the family food bill

*Adult add-on* = Ingredients that might not be suitable for weaning babies but may be added to the recipe if cooking for the sophisticated palate

*Health* = Certain foods have properties that may impact your child's health. For example, there are foods that are soothing for teething babies and those that may aggravate reflux

*Development* = Some ingredients have been highlighted due to their benefits for your child's development, for example those that might boost the immune system or be key in cerebral development

We hope that the addition of these references will be helpful when you decide what recipes and foods to offer your child.

Finally, if you favour precision cooking, please note that 'a glug' corresponds to approximately 2tbsp, 'a squidge' is around 1tbsp and 'a splash' is roughly 50ml.

Chapter One

# About Baby-Led Weaning (BLW)

## What Is Baby-Led Weaning?

Baby-led weaning (BLW) is when you offer solid foods to your baby and allow him to feed himself. This differs to the more traditional method of weaning where you spoon-feed your baby puréed and mashed foods.

## Why Should I BLW?

- Babies gain independence by exploring food for themselves, at their own pace, making mealtimes more fun
- Babies are exposed to many different tastes and textures of food from the start
- Finger foods encourage babies to chew, bite and suck, which helps develop the muscles used for speech
- Self-feeding can improve hand-eye coordination
- Babies are potentially more open to trying new textures and tastes as they continue to grow
- Babies are less likely to become bored and frustrated at mealtimes as they are feeding themselves
- Baby-led weaning will save you time: you need only make one meal as your baby eats what you and the rest of the family eat, meaning they become easily integrated into family mealtimes from the moment you start weaning
- Babies develop healthy eating habits as they learn to self-regulate their feeding. They decide the pace and amount they eat based on their own individual requirements

## Why Shouldn't I Try BLW?

If your baby was born prematurely; is unable to pick up food to bring to his mouth or has difficulty chewing; or there is a family history of food intolerances, allergies or digestive problems, you should contact your GP or health visitor to discuss BLW before trying it.

## When Should I Start Weaning?

There are two approaches for when to wean: the recommendation from the UK Department of Health (DoH), and the cues your baby gives you that they're ready. Currently, the UK DoH recommends introducing solid foods, on top of breast or formula milk, to your baby at around six months of age. Before this, your baby's digestive system is still developing, and weaning too soon may increase the risk of allergies or infections. However, each child is an amazing, unique individual and your child might be ready to wean a little earlier. Watch for signs that your child may be ready. These include:

- Sitting up with little or no support
- Wanting to chew, putting toys and other objects in his mouth
- Grabbing a handful of your food and popping it in his mouth

If you do decide to wean your baby earlier than six months it is advisable to avoid certain foods that may cause adverse reactions (see page 14 for more information on allergies). The DoH guidelines state that solid foods should never be introduced before four months.

## Milk

Initially, food is for fun and exploration, as most of your baby's nourishment will continue to come from breast or formula milk. However, at around six months of age babies begin to need more nourishment than from milk alone. By nine months your baby has probably got the hang of feeding himself a little better and so most of his nutritional needs will be met by food rather than milk. As your baby eats more solids he will naturally take less milk. By reducing the supply to meet the demand you will find your baby will, over time, wean himself from milk feeds. There is no right or wrong time to stop giving milk to your baby. As a guideline, you should continue to offer 500–600ml a day up to the age of twelve months. Follow your instincts and you can't go wrong (but if you do need a little more advice, contact your health visitor or GP).

Cow's milk should be avoided as a drink for babies less than twelve months old since it is lacking in the necessary iron and vitamins found in breast or formula milk. Cooking with cow's milk is suitable for children of any age. As a rule, only use full-fat milk, as this will provide optimum nutrition for your baby.

## Food Groups

At around nine months, it's time to think about balancing your baby's diet to ensure he receives all the nutrients needed for a healthy start. For the first six months, all of these will have come from milk. Nutrients are the building blocks that your baby will use to grow and develop so offering your baby a variety of foods will ensure he has the raw materials with which to build a healthy body.

Nutritional requirements are higher on a per-kilogram basis during infancy and child-hood than at any other developmental stage in life. Your baby's body is growing quickly and so it needs all the nutrients that food can provide to do just that.

Carbohydrates, proteins and fats are essential for growth and healing. Deficits of any of these may compromise these processes and may result in poor health. Offering your child a well-balanced diet with foods from different groups will help give your child the best possible chance of reaching optimum health.

*Carbohydrates:* These are your baby's main source of energy and come in two forms: sugar and starch. Sugar is broken down quickly and gives a near immediate hit of energy whereas starch provides a much slower release. Fruits are a good example of a quick-releasing sugar and potatoes are an example of a slower-releasing starch. Natural sugars can be found in fruit, vegetables and their juices. Natural starches include whole-grain breakfast cereals, bread, pasta and lentils.

*Proteins:* These are needed for the growth and repair of body tissues. Children have a lot of growing to do and so will need more protein in their diet than adults. Proteins can be found in animal products such as meat, fish and cheese. Protein also comes in the form of grains, pulses, nuts and seeds. However, these are only partial proteins and don't contain as many of the essential amino acids found in animal-based proteins.

*Fats:* These are vital for helping the brain and nerves develop, and they provide the most concentrated source of energy. Babies need a higher proportion of fat than adults in their diet. There are two types of fat: saturated fats (that are solid at room temperature) and unsaturated fats (that are liquid at room temperature). Saturated fats, such as butter and lard, come from animal sources. Unsaturated fats mostly come from vegetables, such as avocado, but can also be found in oily fish.

Omega-3 and omega-6 are two types of essential fatty acid and both are key to your baby's brain and visual development. Omega-3 is found in oily fish such as mackerel, tuna and salmon. Omega-6 is found in many cooking oils such as sunflower and corn oil.

*Vitamins and Minerals:* These are nutrients that your body needs in small amounts. There are two types of vitamin: water-soluble and fat-soluble.

Water-soluble vitamins (B6 and B12) can't be stored in the body so should ideally be eaten on a daily basis. Foods such as fruit and vegetables contain most of these vitamins, however, they are easily destroyed by heat. The best way to keep the vitamins in foods is to steam, grill or eat them raw. Avoid boiling, as most vitamins will be lost in the water.

Fat-soluble vitamins (A, D, E and K) can be stored in the liver and fatty tissues so don't need to be eaten as often as water-soluble vitamins. They are found mainly in fatty foods such as butter, lard, cooking oils and oily fish.

Minerals (calcium and iron) can be found in many different foods such as meat, cereals, fish, dairy, fruit and vegetables.

Breast milk contains everything your baby needs until around six months, when your baby's natural store of nutrients starts to deplete. Breast milk alone lacks enough vitamin D for your baby, so if your child is exclusively breastfed, you should discuss with your health visitor the use of vitamin drops. Most formula milk is fortified with vitamin D, however, if your baby is on less than 500ml per day, vitamin drops should be considered also.

## Foods To Avoid

*Salt:* Salt should be avoided wherever possible. Your baby's kidneys need to work hard to process salt, and too much can damage them. When cooking, experiment with herbs and spices to add flavour instead of reaching for the salt pot.

*Sugar:* Is a source of empty calories and is damaging to teeth, refined sugar is best avoided.

*Honey:* Raw honey may be a source of botulism (a potentially fatal infection). It is best avoided until your baby is over twelve months old.

*Eggs:* May be offered from six months but the yolk and white should be solid. Soft-boiled eggs are suitable from twelve months.

*Choking Hazards:* Whole (or large) pieces of nuts are potentially risky. Because of their shape they may cause choking, so avoid giving to children under five. Cherry tomatoes, grapes and olives should all be cut in half for the same reason. Many fruits contain stones, such as plums and cherries, so remove the stone before offering to your baby.

*A note from Felicity*: As a new mum I read lots of conflicting information about offering my little one starch and cereals. Some sources claim that children are unable to digest starch and cereals until two years old or until all teeth are developed. As parents, we're always making choices, whether it's to have a home birth or to use washable nappies; our lives, circumstances and children are all different and one size doesn't always fit all. I believe in 'everything in moderation' when it comes to feeding my family (unless there is a particular medical reason to cut out a food group) but the choice is ultimately yours.

## Allergies

Waiting until your baby is six months old to start weaning is a positive step to avoiding allergies. If you have a history of allergies in your family, introduce a new food and wait for a few days to spot a reaction before introducing further new foods. When to introduce wheat and gluten is always a source of debate and some experts suggest waiting until your baby is twelve months. There are plenty of wheat- and gluten-free products available in local supermarkets today and, if you're unsure, discuss your concerns with your GP or health visitor.

Many acidic foods, such as citrus fruits and tomato-based sauces can cause an allergy-ring around your baby's bottom. Strawberries, pineapples and grapes may also trigger the rash so avoid the suspect food for a few days and see if it disappears. This rash is often a sign of a temporary intolerance, alerting you that the digestive system isn't quite developed enough to process that food just yet. Allow a few days to pass and try again and always, if in doubt, speak to your GP or health visitor.

*Tip*: Keeping a food diary is a smart way to keep track of when you introduce new foods to your baby. It may help to introduce a new food once every few days so if your baby does have a reaction you can easily identify the trigger food.

*Julia's Tip*: I jotted in my diary what George ate that day so when he developed nappy rash (for apparently no reason) I was able to trace it back to strawberries.

Chapter Two

# Getting Started with BLW

Organization is essential to baby-led weaning. Waking up and realizing you haven't got anything for your little one to eat for breakfast is not a great start to the day. It's not essential, but producing a weekly meal planner may allow you to build your shopping list and ensure everyone has a healthy, balanced meal all the time.

A meal planner can also help save you money. Planning your meals will reduce waste, allowing you to bulk buy ingredients and use up any leftovers.

We have created some example meal planners to give you an idea of meals and snacks you can feed your baby, as well as advice on using leftovers. The three planners are slightly different to reflect the changes in your baby's eating habits as she gets progressively better at feeding herself:

**Early BLW Days:** for when you are first starting to wean your baby

At this stage you are probably just placing some of your food on her tray as opposed to cooking her own individual meal (unless you want to freeze portions). For this reason, the shopping list is based on two hearty adult portions (depending on your appetite there may be a small portion left over to freeze).

The meal suggestions contain foods that are easily grasped in the fist of a little one. When you first start to wean your baby she will use her whole hand to grab food (the palmer grasp) to take to her mouth as opposed to using her finger and thumb, as her pincer grip has not yet developed. Foods need to be thick and long enough to be held in her fist with an end to chew on. Soft foods will often be squashed in her fist initially as she will be unaware of her own strength. Your baby will be very curious about the food and will play with it, exploring its feel. She may not eat a lot at the beginning.

**Monday**
L/O Beef rissoles
vegetable and roasted
butternut squash

**Tuesday**
Fish, chips
and peas!

**Wednesday**
Lentil Bolognese
vegetables and roasted
sweet potato

**Thursday**
L/O Lasagne and
potato salad

**Friday**
Easy cheesy pasta
and potato wedges

**Saturday**
L/O Tuna pasta bake
and broccoli

**Sunday**
Slow roast
beef brisket,
vegetables, roasted
sweet potato and
meat stock gravy

| | Monday | Tuesday | Wednesday | Thursday | Friday | Saturday | Sunday |
|---|---|---|---|---|---|---|---|
| **Breakfast** | Slice of buttered Toast (p.38) plus chunks of one of the following Fresh Seasonal Fruits (pp.44–5): melon, banana, grated apple, chunky apple | Natural Fruity Yoghurt (p.171) and chunks of Fresh Seasonal Fruit (pp.44–5) | Buttered Toast (p.38) plus chunks of Fresh Seasonal Fruit (pp.44–5) | Porridge (p.33) with chunks of Fresh Seasonal Fruit (pp.44–5) | Breakfast Cereal (p.37) with chunks of Fresh Seasonal Fruit (pp.44–5) | Natural Fruity Yoghurt (p.171) and chunks of Fresh Seasonal Fruit (pp.44–5) | Buttered Toast (p.38) plus chunks of Fresh Seasonal Fruit (pp.44–5) |
| **Snack** | | | | | | | |
| **Lunch** | Vegetables from Rainbow Salad (p.211) | Rice crackers and Guacamole (p.140) | L/o Rainbow Salad and l/o Guacamole | (Using l/o Porridge p.33) Porridge Pancakes (p.34) | Potato Salad (p.212) | Rice crackers and cheese | Tricolour Salad (p.209) |
| **Snack** | | | | | | | |
| **Dinner** | Fish Fingers (p.55) with Sweet Potato Wedges (p.201), carrots and green beans | Slow Roast Beef Brisket (p.164) with broccoli, roasted sweet potato and cauliflower | (Using l/o Slow Roast Beef Brisket) Beef Rissoles (p.112) with roasted butternut squash, green beans and Sweet Potato Wedges (p.201) | Cauliflower and Broccoli Cheese (p.88) with l/o roasted vegetables | Easy-Cheesy Pasta (p.92) with Sweet Potato Wedges (p.201) | Chicken Skewers (p.105) with l/o Potato Salad | Tuna Pasta Bake (p.99) with l/o Tricolour Salad |
| **Snack** | | | | | | | |
| **Notes** | If you have a family history of allergies then it's best to avoid strawberries until after twelve months as they're a common intolerance | It is a good idea to keep a food journal so you can note what your child likes/dislikes but also to use as a reference point for any reactions | Flavour and texture are symbiotic so exposing your children to a greater variety of textures will increase their acceptance of different flavours | Try to give your baby foods that are easy to grab | | | Many food intolerances will show in four days so today is a good day to alter your breakfast fruit |

Early BLW Days Shopping List: for two adults (and possibly some for the freezer)

| Veggies/Fruit | Meat/Fish/Poultry | Chilled Goods | Pantry |
|---|---|---|---|
| Melon x1 | White fish fillets (skinless, boneless) x2 | Full-fat natural yoghurt x360ml | Loaf of bread (white or brown) |
| Apple x6 | Beef brisket x1kg | Full-fat milk x1.14l | Jumbo (porridge) oats x80g |
| Banana x6 | Boneless, skinless chicken thigh fillets x500g | Crème fraiche x80ml | Breakfast cereal x80g |
| Lettuce (Romaine) x1 | | Cheddar cheese x250g | Tinned sweetcorn x200g |
| Cucumber x1 | | Fresh mozzarella x125g | Rice crackers (small packet) |
| Cherry tomatoes x500g | | Soft cream cheese x25g | Flaked almonds x50g |
| Tomatoes x2 | | Unsalted butter | Free range eggs x4 |
| Cooked beetroot x250g | | | Plain flour x100g |
| | | **Frozen Goods** | Chives (handful) |
| Orange pepper x1 | | Frozen peas x50g | Dried pasta x300g |
| Avocado x2 | | Frozen sweetcorn x50g | Beef stock x100ml |
| Garlic x1 bulb | | | Cooking oil |
| Lemon x1 | | | Olive oil |
| New potatoes x500g | | | Ground black pepper |
| Baking potatoes x1.5kg | | | Mixed herbs (dried) |
| Sweet potato x4 (medium) | | | Fresh basil x30g |
| Celery stalks x2 | | | Ground nutmeg |
| Radishes x4 | | | Tinned tuna x200g |
| Carrots x8 | | | |
| Green beans x200g | | | |
| Broccoli x1 | | | |
| Cauliflower x1 | | | |

**Later BLW Days**: for when your little one is getting the hang of things

This weekly meal planner is ideal for when your child has started to get the hang of feeding herself, for example, she may grab food without squashing too much of it, she will be better at getting food into her mouth and is able to chew. This planner suggests offering foods of different textures and sizes for your child to experience and to allow her the opportunity to develop the pincer grip. Continue to offer food that she can grab with her hands easily to prevent her from becoming frustrated. With her stomach now slightly larger and her appetite increasing, this shopping list is based on cooking for two adults and one small child.

| | Monday | Tuesday | Wednesday | Thursday | Friday | Saturday | Sunday |
|---|---|---|---|---|---|---|---|
| **Breakfast** | Breakfast Bar (p.43) and chunks of Fresh Seasonal Fruit (pp.44–5) | Breakfast Cereal (p.37) and chunks of Fresh Seasonal Fruit (pp.44–5) | Natural Fruity Yoghurt (p.171) and chunks of Fresh Seasonal Fruit (pp.44–5) | Porridge (p.33) and chunks of Fresh Seasonal Fruit (pp.44–5) | Breakfast Cereal (p.37) and chunks of Fresh Seasonal Fruit (pp.44–5) | Toast (p.38) served with Fruit Compote (p.35) | Natural Fruity Yoghurt (p.171) and chunks of Fresh Seasonal Fruit (pp.44–5) |
| **Snack** | | | | | | | |
| **Lunch** | Pitta Pizza (p.54) and salad vegetables | Cheese Sandwich (p.52) and salad vegetables | (using l/o Mama's Lasagne) Meat Balls (p.94) | Poached Egg (p.41) on Toast (p.38) | Broccoli and Cheese Muffins (p.50) | (Using l/o Guacamole) Sandwich (p.52) and Egg Salad (p.210) | (using l/o Fish Fingers and l/o Egg Salad) Fish Cakes (p.154) and Egg Salad (p.210) |
| **Snack** | | | | | | | |
| **Dinner** | Lemon Chicken Stir Fry (p.156) with noodles | Mama's Lasagne (p.121) with any l/o salad vegetables | Turkey Burgers (p.56) in a bun with Sweet Potato Wedges (p.201) and salad vegetables | (Using l/o Turkey Burgers) Turkey Meatloaf (p.57) with roasted vegetables and baked potato | Chicken Fajitas (p.137) with Guacamole (p.140) and Salsa (p.139) | Cauliflower and Broccoli Cheese (p.88) with Fish Fingers (p.55) | Lamb Stew (p.93) with couscous and green beans |

## Later BLW Days Shopping List: for two adults and one small child

| Veggies/Fruit | Meat/Fish/Poultry | Chilled Goods | Pantry |
|---|---|---|---|
| Fresh Seasonal fruit for 6 breakfasts | Beef mince x500g | Full-fat milk x1.42l | Loaf of bread (white or brown) |
| Whole cucumber x1 | Minced turkey x400g | Cheddar cheese x350g | Pitta bread x6 |
| Medium sized parsnips x3 (to roast) | Chicken breast or boneless, skinless chicken thigh fillets x1kg | Full-fat natural yoghurt x360ml | Soft buns x3 |
| Mushrooms x4 | Lamb (shoulder, shank or leg) x1kg | Ricotta cheese x250g | Tortilla wraps x5 (white or brown) |
| Lime x1 | Fillet of white fish (skinless & boneless) x1 | Mozzarella cheese x125g | Free range eggs x6 |
| Lemon x1 | | Parmesan cheese x25g | |
| Apple x1 | | Unsalted butter | Fresh coriander bunch |
| Cherry tomatoes x500g | | | Green chilli x2 |
| Lettuce x1 | | | Garlic bulb x1 |
| Butternut squash x1 (to roast) | | | Fresh ginger (small piece) |
| Bag of rocket | | | Rice x500g |
| Medium sized carrots x3 (to roast) | | | Noodles (dried) x120g |
| Tomatoes x4 | | | Couscous x 500g |
| Avocado x3 | | | Self-raising flour x200g |
| Onion x4 | | | Plain flour x50g |
| Red onion x1 | | | Lasagne sheets x12 |
| Leek x1 | | | Porridge oats x500g |
| Peppers x4 | | | Breakfast cereal x40g |
| Baking potatoes x6 | | | Dried apricots x50g |
| Broccoli head x1 | | | Dried prunes x50g |
| Cauliflower x1 | | | Raisins or sultanas x50g |
| Green beans x1 pack | | | Olive oil |
| Shallot x1 | | | Tinned tuna or salmon x200g |
| Lemongrass x1 small packet | | | Tomato purée x6tbsp |
| Mange tout x180g | | | Oregano (dried) |
| Baby corn x175g | | | Cayenne pepper |
| Salad vegetables x3 meals | | | Basil (dried) |
| | | | Mild chilli powder |
| | | | Black pepper |
| | | | Cinnamon (ground) |
| | | | Coriander (dried) |
| | | | Runny honey x 2tbsp |
| | | | Chicken stock x150ml |
| | | | Cornflour x1tbsp |
| | | | Chopped tomatoes, 5 x400g tins |

**Established BLW Days**: For when your child is happily feeding herself

At around nine months you may find your child is quite happily feeding herself and is eating rather than just playing with her food. You may notice that her pincer grip is improving so she can easily pick up small pieces of food with her finger and thumb and can release food as well as grab it (so you may find food being dropped on the floor!). This meal planner offers a variety of foods and explores an array of textures, tastes, sizes and shapes, which enable your child to continue her exciting exploration of the wonderful world of food. Snacks have now been included as before this time you may have been offering your child milk feeds in between mealtimes. As your child continues to grow they will become more active and snacks can be an important part of their diet, aiding this development. In fact, you may find that your child eats better little and often as opposed to having three main meals a day, which is why it's just as important to think about the nutritional value of the snacks you are offering as it is to consider the food you're serving at mealtimes. In this planner we have given you an idea as to some healthy snacks. The shopping list is based on cooking for two adults and one small child.

| | Monday | Tuesday | Wednesday | Thursday | Friday | Saturday | Sunday |
|---|---|---|---|---|---|---|---|
| **Breakfast** | Natural Fruity Yoghurt (p.171) and chunks of Fresh Seasonal Fruit (pp.44–5) | Poached Egg (p.41) on Toast (p.38) | Porridge (p.33) and chunks of Fresh Seasonal Fruit (pp.44–5) | Drop Scones (p.42) with chunks of Fresh Seasonal Fruit (pp.44–5) | Breakfast Cereal (p.37) with chunks of Fresh Seasonal Fruit (pp.44–5) | Breakfast Quinoa (p.46) with Toast (p.38) | Toast (p.38) with Fruit Compote (p.35) |
| **Snack** | | Raw Veggie Sticks (p.31) | | Raisins | | Banana Bread (p.194) | |
| **Lunch** | Sandwich (p.52) with tuna, cucumber and salad vegetables | Raw Veggie Sticks (p.31) with hummus and Guacamole (p.140) | (Using l/o leek) Leek and Potato Soup (p.66) with Wholemeal Bread Sticks (p.193) | Cheese and Tomato Tartlet (p.61) with salad vegetables | (Using l/o pastry) Cheesy Pastry Bites (p.60) with l/o salad vegetables | L/o Garlic Bread with Tricolour Salad (p.209) | Cheese Sandwich (p.52) and Roasted Veggie Sticks (p.31) |
| **Snack** | Chunks of Fresh Seasonal Fruit (pp.44–5) | | Oaty Fruity Biscuits (p.199) | | L/o Wholemeal Bread Sticks | | Chunks of Fresh Seasonal Fruit (pp.44–5) |
| **Dinner** | Fakeaway night – Mum's Chicken Curry (p.144) with rice | Lamb Roast Dinner (p.165) with roast potatoes, leeks, carrots, peas and cabbage | (Using l/o lamb) Lamb Couscous Salad (p.110) | Vegetarian Moussaka (p.79) with steamed cabbage and carrots | Meaty Bolognese (p.125) with Garlic Bread (p.120) | (Using l/o Meaty Bolognese) Pizza Bolognese (p.77) with l/o Tricolour Salad | Penny's Salmon Quinoa (p.214) and salad |

Established BLW Days Shopping List roughly feeds two adults and one little one

| Veggies/Fruit | Meat/Fish/Poultry | Chilled Goods | Pantry |
|---|---|---|---|
| Fresh Seasonal fruit for x5 breakfasts and x2 snacks | Lamb shoulder x1.5kg | Full-fat natural yoghurt x500ml | Fresh ginger (small) |
| Apple x1 | Chicken breasts or skinless, boneless chicken thigh fillets x500g | Apple juice x25ml | Garlic bulb x2 |
| Lemons x2 | Mince beef or turkey x400g | Mozzarella cheese x125g | Green chilli x1 |
| Bananas x3 | | Cheddar cheese x200g | Fresh coriander bunch |
| Bunch of celery | | Parmesan cheese x60g | Fresh rosemary bunch |
| Cherry tomatoes x500g | | Hummus x200g | Fresh mint bunch |
| Avocado x4 | | Unsalted butter | Fresh parsley bunch |
| Lettuce x1 | | | Free range eggs x4 |
| Cucumber x1 | | | Full-fat milk x570ml |
| Peppers x3 | | | |
| Spring onion bunch | | **Frozen** | Raisins or sultanas x50g |
| Mushrooms x6 | | Bag of frozen peas | Dried apricots x50g |
| Leeks x4 | | | Dried prunes x50g |
| Baking potatoes x5 | | | Olive oil |
| Spinach x100g | | | Loaf of bread (wholemeal) |
| Aubergine x1 | | | Baguette x1 |
| Onions x4 | | | Tinned puy or green lentils x400g |
| Carrots x4 | | | Coconut milk x400ml |
| Small white cabbage x1 | | | Salt-free pizza base x1 |
| Salad vegetables x3 meals | | | Puff pastry pack x1 |
| | | | Chopped tomatoes, 4 x400g tins |
| | | | Porridge oats x40g |
| | | | Tinned tuna x200g |
| | | | Tinned red salmon x200g |
| | | | Dried spaghetti x225g |
| | | | Breakfast cereal |
| | | | Wholemeal bread flour x450g |
| | | | Fast-action dried yeast x7g |
| | | | Quinoa x150g |
| | | | Ground cinnamon |
| | | | Ground cumin |
| | | | Ground coriander |
| | | | Turmeric |
| | | | Paprika |
| | | | Ground nutmeg |
| | | | Tomato purée x2tbsp |
| | | | Malt vinegar x2tbsp |
| | | | Plain flour x6tbsp |
| | | | Ground black pepper |
| | | | Self-raising flour x6tbsp |
| | | | Chicken stock x220ml |

## Feeding Equipment

*Highchair:* Baby-led weaning is messy so invest in a plastic, easy-to-clean type such as the Ikea Antilop. If your baby is slumped in the chair, pop a rolled-up towel behind her back so she is closer to the table. If you can, position the highchair so the back is against a wall. It will help reduce the chance of your little one kicking the chair over. Your baby will want to copy you so ideally have your baby eating from a plate at the table rather than the highchair tray.

> ***Emma's tip****: Instead of buying a stand-alone highchair we decided to purchase a travel highchair. It was ideal for transporting, fitted perfectly onto our dining room chairs and was cheaper than many stand-alone highchairs. It meant our son was at the ideal height for the table and was easily integrated at family mealtimes.*

*Long-sleeved bibs:* It's easier to bung these straight in the washing machine after each meal, so invest in several. Choose bibs with elasticated wrists, otherwise one day you will think your baby has eaten lots only to discover it all hiding up her sleeve. Avoid those with poppers at the neck, as these are a potential choking hazard.

*Pelican bibs:* Wipe-clean and great at catching any dropped crumbs. Wear over a long-sleeved bib and soon your baby will realize it catches her food and pick it out.

*Wipe-clean tablecloth:* Save the fabric tablecloth for a special occasion and use a PVC or disposable tablecloth, or oilcloth instead. It makes clearing up that bit easier.

*PVC Sheet:* To avoid mopping the floor after every meal, lay some cheap PVC under the highchair to catch spills. A cheap shower curtain is ideal.

*Doidy Cup:* This tilted beaker with handles is great for serving drinks.

*Plastic and metal weaning spoons:* Some babies want a spoon, others want to use their fingers and you may even have one who only uses a spoon on a Friday. Your baby naturally wants to copy you so have some cutlery to hand, just in case it's one of those days. If your baby takes to the spoon, a rubber tipped spoon may be better suited for their sensitive gums.

*Wipes, kitchen roll and muslins:* For cleaning up a messy face and hands after the meal have plenty of wipes, kitchen roll or damp muslins to hand.

## Safety First

Before you start BLW, some do's and don'ts:

- Don't let anyone, except your baby, put food in their mouth
- Don't leave your baby alone with food
- Don't give your baby any salt, sugar or whole nuts
- Don't give your baby any raw honey until they're twelve months old
- Do make sure your baby is sitting upright to eat
- Do cut small fruits such as grapes and cherries in half and remove any stones
- Do be prepared for a mess
- Do be prepared to have some fun!

## The First Time

Baby-led weaning is not for the faint-hearted. It can be a messy process but it will give you enormous pleasure to watch your little one making choices and eating independently. Be prepared for strangers to come up to you and say, "Oh look, your little one is eating broccoli" and for your family and friends to be astonished (and opinionated). It will improve your baby's hand-eye coordination and free your hands up to eat your own food. But there is a downside: it will mean you will miss out on making those aeroplane noises as you try and shovel another spoonful of food into a clamped mouth. Oh, and don't forget the mess!

Begin by offering food once a day when you have plenty of time. Choose a time when your baby is not too tired or hungry as they may become irritable. Lunchtime is often a good time as they're not full up from a morning milk feed and will have expended plenty of energy on that morning's activities.

## Getting Started with BLW:

- Position plenty of wipes and kitchen roll nearby
- Have all your child's food and drink to hand before you start, so you don't have to keep nipping to the fridge
- Have something for yourself at the same time. You may be sat there for a while and your baby will be more inclined to tuck in and copy you
- Lay some cheap PVC matting or newspaper on the floor around the highchair
- Pop your baby in the highchair, placing a rolled-up towel behind her back if she's too far away from the table
- Dress your baby in a long-sleeved bib with a pelican bib on top
- Place some food on the table and watch them explore. Some suitable first foods are suggested on pages 29–31

It's as simple as that. Remember, you are offering your baby the chance to try some food, you are not feeding them. If they're not interested, don't worry and try again at the next mealtime.

Throughout weaning, continue to offer regular milk feeds and gradually your baby will reduce her milk intake as her appetite for food grows.

The importance of allowing your baby to feed herself cannot be stressed enough. Research has shown that higher-than-recommended energy intakes in children as young as four months have been shown to predict a greater risk of obesity in childhood and adulthood. From the moment you wean, by selecting foods with nutritional value you are allowing your child from this young age to make decisions about which healthy foods she will select from those you make available to her. You are already setting your child on the path to a lifetime of healthy eating.

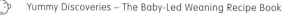

## Is My Child Eating Enough?

Once your baby gets used to her one lunchtime meal per day, gradually increase it to two then three meals a day over several weeks. Take the lead from your baby as to how much to serve and, if she still seems hungry after her feast, offer a little more but remember you are offering not obliging her to eat. As time goes on, she will naturally increase her food and start to reduce her milk intake. Each baby will take a different amount of time to get the hang of eating so don't rush the process or be tempted to try and keep up with other mummies; eating is a skill and it takes time, practice and patience.

At nine months, the DoH recommends your baby should be eating three balanced meals a day in addition to 500–600ml of breast or formula milk. She should, on a daily basis, be enjoying:

- Three to four servings of carbohydrates
- Three to four servings of fruit and vegetables
- Two servings of protein

But what is a serving? A good guide is to think of a serving as 1tbsp for each year of age. A rough daily guide might be:

| 1 year old | 2 year old | 3 year old |
|---|---|---|
| 3–4tbsp fruit or veg | 6–8tbsp fruit or veg | 9–12tbsp fruit or veg |
| 2tbsp protein | 4tbsp protein | 6tbsp protein |
| 3–4tbsp bread or cereal | 6–8tbsp bread or cereal | 8–12tbsp bread or cereal |

Remember, this is over the course of an entire day. Your stomach is around the size of your fist so compare the size of your child's fist against yours and you will see how different children will have different appetites.

*Sam's Tip*: By having a meal planner for Imogen it ensured I covered the food groups each day and helped me track what she liked and disliked.

## Cheeky Storage – The Hamster Trick

Some babies like to tuck a piece of food away in their cheek for later. This may not happen until your baby has better tongue control so once she starts sticking her tongue out you might want to consider checking at the end of each meal. Running your little finger around the inside of her cheeks or giving a drink at the end of the meal can help clear the mouth, especially if your baby likes spitting the water back into the cup.

## Gagging and Choking

It is very unlikely that a baby would choke doing BLW as initially only large pieces of food should be served. If your baby isn't developmentally ready to swallow then it is unlikely she will be able to bite off a choke-size chunk and move it to the back of her mouth to swallow it – a sort of natural protection. Choking is more likely when feeding children with a spoon or putting small finger foods into their mouths for them.

Whilst your baby is working out how to swallow food she may occasionally gag and vomit. The gag reflex is there to prevent things being swallowed which ought not to be. In younger babies the gag reflex 'trigger zone' is a lot further forward in the mouth than in adults as a way of preventing them from swallowing toys and other objects which often go in their mouth as a way of learning. With it being so far forward it is natural that spoons, little fingers and first foods will trigger this reflex and so gagging is likely to occur when you first start weaning. The first time it happens you will probably be more alarmed than your little one but chances are she will probably just spit out the food and carry on without being bothered by it at all. Remember, children are very in-tune with your body language and emotions so even if you are panicking inside, try and remain calm.

The gag reflex in adults is often triggered voluntarily as a way of trying to induce vomiting. You may have heard this referred to as 'sticking your fingers down your throat'. If you've ever had to do this, you will know that the reflex is quite far back (roughly the length of your index finger) but it took time and practice for that reflex 'trigger zone' to recede all that way and your baby is working on that through weaning.

Swallow. Have you ever thought about how many muscles in coordination are needed to do that? It takes practice to work out how to move the food with the tongue to the back of the throat and coordinate all those tiny muscles to enable the swallowing action, and your child will make mistakes. But that's how we learn. Eventually she will work out how to get the right-sized food to the correct part of her mouth and it will get easier to co-ordinate all of those muscles. Then that gag reflex will no longer be as necessary and it will start to recede as you watch your little one become an efficient eater.

Avoid offering food to your child when she's lying back in a car seat. To ensure the gag reflex is triggered, your little one needs to be sitting upright so when food does hit the trigger zone it can be moved forward either to be chewed some more or spat out.

Choking is another matter entirely and involves the airway itself being (partially) blocked – so the food is now beyond the gag reflex. There is no reason that your child should be more likely to choke with BLW, so long as you follow the basic guidelines. See page 14 for more information on choking hazards. Remember: Never leave your baby alone with food.

> **Sarah's tip**: I attended a children's first aid course run by my local children's centre so if William did choke I knew I would be prepared.

## Clearing Up

Pop the plates and cutlery out of reach then, with a wipe, clean your baby's hands and face. Remove the bibs, sweeping any food from the table on to the floor. Take your little one out of the highchair and dust any food in the chair onto the floor before finally clearing up the floor with a dishcloth. Pop the cloth and bib into the washing machine and get a fresh one ready for the next meal.

Your baby will probably have a wet nappy about twenty minutes after drinking so it might be worth delaying a nappy change until then.

BLW is a messy process so you and your baby may from time to time encounter food stains, especially from tomato-based sauces. We've found these tips for preventing stains useful.

- Soak the item in cold water as soon as possible

- Sunlight can be effective. Wash the item and leave it to dry in a conservatory or greenhouse for a few days and the stain may miraculously disappear

- Try boiling clothes on the stove with a little washing powder

- If all else fails, try adding a stain remover to your next load of washing

Chapter Three

# First Foods

The development of the nervous system means that, at weaning age, babies are initially only able to hold things in their fists, as their pincer grasp has not yet developed. Serving up easy-to-handle foods is a good way to get started with this exciting milestone.

You are going to be understandably nervous the first time you give your child solid food. To help you get started we've outlined some suggestions on what to serve up for your first meal:

*Steamed or boiled veggie sticks*
Wash, then steam or boil for about ten minutes.

- Broccoli florets
- Cauliflower florets

*Roasted veggie sticks*
Wash, peel and cut into big sticks, chunks or wedges. Roast in some olive oil in the oven on 190C/170C fan/gas 5, for about 30 minutes. A rough size can be seen on page 31.

- Sweet potato
- Butternut squash
- Parsnips
- Carrots

*Raw fruit and veggie sticks*
Taste the food before giving it to your child in case you have an orange that's a little tart or a plum that's a bit hard or even what you thought were seedless grapes turning out to be seeded!

If your baby sees you eating the same foods he'll be more inclined to want to copy you and eat the same things so sit down and enjoy your meal together.

- Fresh Pineapple – chop the skin off and then cut into big chunks
- Melon – remove the skin and pips and then cut into chunks
- Cucumber – your choice whether to peel or not, wash and cut into big pieces
- Strawberries – wash and serve whole if nice and big
- Banana – peel and serve whole
- Peaches; nectarines; plums – peel, cut into quarters and remove the stone
- Pear – choose a soft pear, peel or wash and cut into chunks

For more ideas on serving fruit to your baby see Fresh Seasonal Fruit (page 44–5).

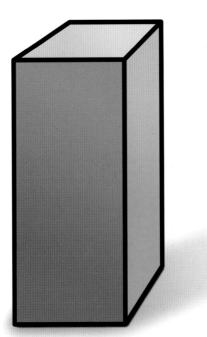

Chapter Four

# Breakfast

Initially, your baby may not be interested in breakfast, happier instead with a milk feed. When you do introduce breakfast, get organized the night before. The last thing you want is to wake in the morning and have nothing to offer. From experience, be assured that turning up at the petrol station in your pyjamas buying milk and bread is not a good look. Initially, avoid giving really messy foods at breakfast, such as yoghurt and runny porridge as they can take longer to clear up.

If you eat breakfast, you may find that you eat the same thing daily so be sure to vary your diet. Your baby wants to copy you so sitting down and eating common foods at breakfast together will encourage your baby to sample new foods.

# Porridge

Preparation Time: 5 minutes
Cooking Time: 5 minutes
**Serves 1 little person**

## Ingredients

40g porridge oats
Few glugs of full-fat milk

**TO SERVE:** Fruit Purée (page 36); Fruit Compote (page 35); blueberries; strawberries; banana; raisins

## Method

1. Prepare the porridge on the stove or in the microwave, following the instructions on the box
2. Stir in some fresh fruit such as chopped blueberries, blackberries, strawberries or some raisins. Alternatively try a dollop of Fruit Purée (page 36) or Fruit Compote (page 35)

---

*Tip*: Make the porridge thick and stodgy so your little one can pick it up with their fingers. Once they're better at using the spoon, you can start to experiment with consistency.

*Adult add-on*: Experiment with toppings such as a dollop of Greek yoghurt, runny honey, brown sugar or some flaked almonds.

*Leftovers*: Use porridge to make Porridge Pancakes (page 34) or Sleepy-Pud (page 190).

*Development*: The brain needs a constant supply of energy and the oats' slow-release of glucose helps with its high demands.

*Development*: Eating blueberries can improve short-term memory as well as enhance balance and coordination in your rapidly developing baby.

*Health*: Porridge is high in fibre, which may help relieve the symptoms of constipation.

# Porridge Pancakes

Preparation Time: 5 minutes
Cooking Time: 5 minutes
**50g of leftover porridge
 makes 2 large pancakes**

## Ingredients
*Leftover Porridge (page 33)
*Plain flour
*Full-fat milk
1 egg
1tsp unsalted butter
(*for every 100g leftover porridge add 50ml milk and 50g flour)

**TO SERVE:** Fruit Purée (page 36); Fruit Compote (page 35)

## Method

1.  Mix the ingredients together to form a stiff batter – the mixture should cling to a spoon. To thicken add more flour or oats and to thin add more milk
2.  Melt the butter in a frying pan over a medium heat
3.  Spoon a blob of mixture into the pan and roll it around, coating the base
4.  Flip the pancake over when browned to cook the other side so the mixture is firm and not sticky

> **Health**: Avoid giving milky food when your little one has a cold as it may help stimulate mucus production. Be sure to continue with milk feeds.

# Fruit Compote

Preparation Time: 5 minutes
Cooking Time: 20 minutes
**Serves 1 grown-up and 1 little person**

## Ingredients

Seasonal fruit e.g. apples, pears, cherries, plums
1 handful of dried apricots
1 handful of dried prunes
Splash of water
Splash of prune juice (optional)

**TO SERVE:** Toast (page 38); Natural Fruity Yoghurt (page 171); Porridge (page 33)

## Method

1. Wash the fruit and remove any stones, peeling if needed
2. Pop in a saucepan with enough water so the fruit is covered
3. Put on a low heat on the stove so it's just bubbling for around 20 minutes or until the fruit is soft and squidgy, adding more water if necessary

> *Tip*: This recipe is ideal for using up old fruit ageing in your fridge or fruit bowl, or if you have an abundance from blackberry or apple picking
> *Health*: We call this recipe 'The dam buster'. Serve to your constipated child and watch the movement!
> *Leftovers*: Use to make Fruit Jelly (page 185) or Oaty Fruity Biscuits (page 199).

# Fruit Purée

Preparation Time: 5 minutes
**Serves 1 grown-up and 1 little person**

## Ingredients

Seasonal soft fruit e.g. strawberries, raspberries,
  blueberries, blackberries, peaches, or nectarines

**TO SERVE:** Toast (page 38); Natural Fruity Yoghurt (page 171); Porridge (page 33)

## Method

1. Wash the fruit and remove any stones, peeling if necessary
2. Squidge with a potato masher or whizz for a few seconds in a food blender

---

*Leftovers*: Mix in with Fruit Jelly (page 185) or Oaty Fruity Biscuits (page 199).
**Health***: Watch for a nappy rash after serving strawberries, as younger children are commonly intolerant to the high acidity. See page 14 for more information on allergies.*
**Wendy's Tip***: For nappy rash I brew a chamomile tea bag in some hot water, add 1tsp of honey, and a couple of drops of lavender and tea tree oil. Then leave to cool and bathe Barney's bottom with it. This has a natural antiseptic and soothing effect on the rash.*

# Breakfast Cereal

Preparation Time: 5 minutes
**Serves 1 little person**

**Ingredients**
Cereal
Full-fat milk

**Method**
1.  Sprinkle a few flakes in a bowl and cover with milk

*Tip*: Specific baby cereals are available, but shop around and you may be surprised at how many cereals are suitable for you both to eat. Read the labels and avoid those with added salt, sugar, nuts and honey.

*Tip*: Recipes are changing and new products are being launched continuously but some examples of appropriate breakfast cereals might include: Weetabix, Bitesize Shredded Wheat, Rice Krispies and Corn Flakes.

*Tip*: Experiment with the texture and consistency of your breakfast cereal. Weetabix with just a few drops of milk is a different experience for your child than when it is soggy. You might also experiment with serving it warm or cold.

*Development*: As your child grows and develops, try introducing a fork or spoon. As she strives to copy you this may well be sooner than you think.

*Health*: Many breakfast cereals are high in fibre, which may help relieve the symptoms of constipation.

*Health*: Often children with recurrent glue ear have an allergy to cow's milk so consider trying goat, rice or buffalo milk as an alternative when cooking or putting on cereal. Remember, these milks should not replace your child's milk feeds as they do not contain adequate nutrition.

*Nicola's Tip*: If Weetabix gets on the floor, walls or table, clear it up quickly before it hardens. It can be tough to scrape off.

# Toast

Cooking Time: 5 minutes
**Serves 1 little person**

## Ingredients
Wholemeal Salt-Free Bread (page 39)

**TO SERVE:** unsalted butter; Fruit Purée (page 36); Fruit Compote (page 35)

## Method
1. Toast the bread in the toaster or under the grill
2. Cut into fingers
3. Serve with your choice of topping

*Tip*: St Dalfour fruit spread is a nice alternative to jam and contains no added sugar. It is available in the preserves section in most major supermarkets.
*Tip*: When buying bread, always read the label. Those labelled 'healthy' may not be as low in salt as you think.
*Tip*: If re-warming toast in the microwave, lean two pieces together to make a tent-shape and use a defrost setting – the lower power should prevent sogginess.
*Tip*: Try rolling the bread with a rolling pin before toasting. It will crispen up, giving your child a different texture on their tongue.
*Leftovers*: Serve with Poached Egg (page 41) or Scrambled Egg (page 40) for a quick lunch. Buttered toast turns nicely into French Toast (page 47).
*Health*: Some babies find the high fibre content of brown bread a bit too much to begin with and have a runny tummy. If this happens, switch to white for a few days and try again.
*Fran's Tip*: When I bake a loaf, I cut off a couple of slices and pop them in the freezer for emergencies. Even if the cupboards are bare I can always serve toast and something!

# Bread Maker Wholemeal Salt-Free Bread

Preparation Time: 5 minutes
Cooking Time: 1–3 hours
**Makes 1 medium-sized loaf**

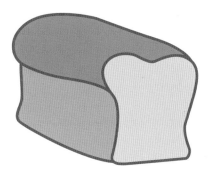

## Ingredients

Bread maker
225ml warm water
Glug of olive oil or sunflower oil
Glug of runny honey
450g strong brown bread flour
1¼tsp dried yeast

## Method

1. Pour all the wet ingredients into the bread maker
2. Add the flour and finally sprinkle in the yeast
3. Set the bread maker to a wholemeal programme and leave to bake

*Leftovers*: Use your freshly baked bread to make Toast (page 38), French Toast (page 47) and Sandwiches (page 52). Home-made bread is preservative-free so doesn't keep as long as shop bought. Use your ageing bread to make breadcrumbs for Fish Fingers (page 55), Chicken and Apple Sausages (page 58) or Chicken Fingers (page 62), alternatively you can freeze your breadcrumbs in a Ziploc bag until needed.

# Scrambled Egg

Preparation Time: 5 minutes
Cooking Time: 5 minutes
**Serves 1 little person**

## Ingredients

1tsp unsalted butter
1 egg
Splash of water or full-fat milk

**TO SERVE:** Toast (page 38)

## Method

**MICROWAVE:**

1.  Using a fork, whisk the ingredients in a microwave-safe bowl and pop in the microwave for 2 minutes. Check and stir every 20–30 seconds until egg mixture has set.

**STOVE:**

1.  Melt the butter in a frying pan on a medium heat
2.  Crack the egg into the frying pan and use a plastic whisk to scramble
3.  Add a splash of water or milk and whisk it all together
4.  Cook and stir for around 5 minutes until the mixture has set

---

*Adult add-on*: Smoked salmon or chorizo make lovely additions to this simple breakfast.
*Leftovers*: Don't throw leftover Scrambled Egg away. Use it with Special Fried Rice (page 153) or Sandwiches (page 52).
*Development*: Eggs contain folate, which helps with growth and maintenance of new cells in the body.

# Poached Egg

Preparation Time: 5 minutes
Cooking Time: 5 minutes
**Serves 1 little person**

## Ingredients
1tsp unsalted butter
1 egg
Egg poacher

**TO SERVE:** Toast (page 38)

## Method
1. Boil a deep pan of water
2. Add the butter to the poacher, crack the egg into it and lower carefully into the water
3. Cover for 5–6 minutes, ensuring the egg white is cooked through

> *Tip*: A microwave egg poacher that poaches the egg in a couple of minutes can be a useful and inexpensive kitchen gadget.
>
> *Tip*: Experiment with the consistency of the egg yolk once your little one is a year old (undercooked eggs can be problematic for very young, delicate tummies). Overcooked egg is easy for your child to pick up with her hands or a fork, whereas a runny yolk is a good dipper for toast (or fingers).
>
> *Development*: Eggs contain vitamin A, which will stimulate your baby's immune system.
>
> *Danielle's Tip*: Poached egg on toast is a favourite quick tea in our house.

# Drop Scones

Preparation Time: 5 minutes
Cooking Time: 15 minutes
**Makes 12–16 small drop scones**

## Ingredients

1tsp unsalted butter
285ml full-fat milk
1 egg
1–2tbsp self-raising flour
1tsp baking powder
Optional: 1tsp cinnamon and a handful of sultanas or blueberries

**TO SERVE:** Fruit Purée (page 36); Fruit Compote (page 35)

## Method

1. Pour the milk into a measuring jug and whisk in the egg and baking powder
2. Add the flour until it is a batter consistency, making up to around 400ml
3. Add the flavour variation of your choice. If freezing, do so now
4. Melt the butter in a frying pan on a medium heat
5. Spoon several small dollops of batter into the pan (you're making mini-pancakes). Once they've firmed up, use a spatula to flip and cook the other side until brown

*Tip*: These make great snacks but beware of stains from blueberries.
**Leftovers**: Before adding the variation, save the batter mix to make Omelette Crêpes (page 51) or Chicken Pancakes (page 114).
**Development**: Milk contains calcium, which is ideal for babies' growing bones and teeth.

# Breakfast Bars

Preparation Time: 5 minutes
Cooking Time: 20 minutes
**Makes 10–12 breakfast bars**

## Ingredients

450g porridge oats
570ml full-fat milk
3 handfuls of raisins or sultanas
Butter for greasing

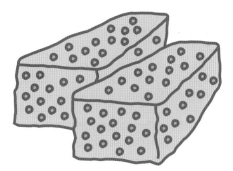

## Method

1.  Preheat the oven to 200C/180C fan/gas 6
2.  Mix all the ingredients together in a bowl
3.  Grease a non-stick baking tin, tip the mixture in and smooth flat
4.  Pop in the oven for 20 minutes or until brown and golden on top
5.  When cooled you can cut into large fingers or bars

*Tip*: These make a great snack and are yummy with Fruit Purée (page 36), or Fruit Compote (page 35) spread on top
*Leftovers*: Crumble the cooked bars and use to make Cheesecake (page 172)

## Fresh Seasonal Fruit

**Grapes**: Select a seedless variety, wash and cut in half before serving to prevent choking.
*Health: Grapes are an ideal energy booster and can help prevent constipation. They are acidic and may trigger nappy rash, a sign your child's digestive system isn't quite ready for this food.*

**Cherries**: Wash, halve and remove the stone before serving.

**Oranges, clementines, satsumas**: Opt for sweet and seedless varieties. Peel and remove pips beforehand.
*Health: Citrus fruits are acidic so look out for a possible reaction that your baby isn't ready just yet. You may see a rash around the mouth or bottom. For more information see Allergies (page 14).*

*Tip: With their bright colour, cherries are an attention-grabber. When choosing cherries, generally the darker the colour the sweeter the taste. The fresher fruit will be shiny and the skin unblemished.*

**Melon**: Buy melon in season for a nicer flavour and less expensive prices. Honeydew is a winter melon; cantaloupe and watermelons are summer varieties. Remove the seeds and peel, serving as a nice big chunk to chomp on.

*Tip: When choosing a melon, thump it with your fingers. If it sounds hollow and smells lovely and 'melon-like' you've probably got a nice, fresh one. Over-ripe or rotting melons will have scratches, bruising and soggy patches.*

**Pineapple**: Peel and serve in big chunks.

*Tip: Pineapples don't ripen once picked, so be sure it's ripe when you buy it. Pull one of the leaves from the crown and if it comes out easily it's ripe.*

*Health: Pineapples are high in acidity. In babies with reflux it's sometimes best avoided until they're little older.*

**Apple**: Wash, grate and pop in a little pile for your little one to help herself. When older, offer bigger chunks to chew on.

*Tip: To store the apple until later, pop in a container and cover with water to prevent browning.*

**Pear**: If soft and squidgy simply wash and let your baby 'gum' on it. If firm, wash and grate in a little pile for self-serving.

*Tip*: Pears take a long time to ripen so pop in a bag with a banana to speed it up but not in the fridge or they'll never ripen. Avoid those with too many brown speckles on the skin as this may affect the flavour

**Banana**: Peel a ripe, soft banana and let your little one help herself.

*Tip*: Once ripe, pop bananas in the fridge. The skin will darken but this won't affect the flavour.

**Strawberries, raspberries, blackberries, blueberries:** Wash and serve as they come.

*Tip*: Watch out for the sizes as some fruits, particularly blueberries, can be quite large or firm so may need to be cut in half to avoid choking.
*Leftovers*: Use leftover or over-ripe fruit to make Fruit Purée (page 36); Fruit Compote (page 35); or Oaty Fruity Bars (page 48).
*Health*: Children are exposed to many bacteria and viruses. Packed with folic acid and vitamin C, berries will help give your child's immune system a boost.
*Liz's Tip*: I never throw fruit away. As it starts to get a little older and squidgy, I mush it up and pop in a Ziploc bag or ice cube tray in the freezer. This is great for defrosting and spreading on Toast (page 38), stirring into Porridge (page 33) or adding to a Smoothie (pages 188–9) or Fruity Cereal Bar (page 198).

# Breakfast Quinoa

Preparation Time: 5 minutes
Cooking Time: 5 minutes
**Serves 1 little person**

## Ingredients

50g quinoa
1 pear or apple
150ml apple juice
Handful of raisins
Pinch of cinnamon
Pinch of nutmeg

## Method

1. Peel, core and dice the pear or apple
2. Tip the quinoa in a small saucepan with the apple juice, pear or apple, raisins, cinnamon and nutmeg
3. Simmer for 5 minutes over a low heat until the fruit is soft and water absorbed

*Tip*: Quinoa is a high-protein food and a great alternative to rice or couscous in any meal.
*Development*: Quinoa contains phosphorous, which makes it important for brain development.
*Development*: The grainy quinoa and gooey fruit make this great for exploring first textures.
*Health*: Pears are the least acidic of all fruits and are a great first food for a refluxy baby. Nutmeg is also known to reduce acidity and is ideal for babies with reflux.

# French Toast

Preparation Time: 5 minutes
Cooking Time: 5 minutes
**Serves 1 little person**

## Ingredients
1tsp unsalted butter
2 eggs
1 slice of Bread (page 39)

**TO SERVE:** Fruit Compote (page 35); Fruit Purée (page 36)

## Method
1. Whisk the eggs together in a bowl
2. Cut the bread into small squares and soak in the egg
3. Melt the butter in a frying pan on a medium heat
4. Pop the bread in the frying pan for several minutes until the egg hardens
5. Flip over and cook until golden brown

---

*Tip:* To make the egg mixture go that little bit further, add a splash of milk in step 1.

*Adult add-on:* For a luxury breakfast use brioche instead of bread. Add to the egg mixture: 1tbsp caster sugar and a drop of vanilla extract. Serve with ice cream and fruit compote for a sweet, delicious breakfast.

*Leftovers:* This can also be served cold, so save any leftovers in the fridge and serve as snacks.

*Leftovers:* Makes a great accompaniment to Banana Ice Cream (page 181) for a yummy dessert.

---

## Oaty Bars

Preparation Time: 5 minutes
Cooking Time: 20 minutes
**Makes 6–8 Oaty Bars**

### Ingredients

100g Oatmeal
2tbsp full-fat natural yoghurt
Big splash of apple juice or grape juice
Optional: berries such as raspberries or
   blueberries, or Fruit Compote (page 35) or Fruit Purée (page 36)

> **Tip**: These make a lovely snack and are nice dipped into yoghurt. Store in a food storage container in the fridge for several days. **Leftovers**: Use any crumbly bits or leftover bars to make Cheesecake (page 172).

### Method

1. Preheat the oven to 180C/160C fan/gas 4
2. Mix the yoghurt and oatmeal together, adding enough apple or grape juice to make it sticky
3. Stir in any optional ingredients. If using berries, squidge with a potato masher first
4. Grease a baking tray with butter then pour in the mixture, smooth and pop in the oven for 20 minutes or until golden brown
5. Remove and allow to cool before cutting into bars.

Chapter Five

# Lunch and Lighter Bites

Lunch for little people isn't necessarily your typical twelve o'clock meal. Lunchtime in our house can be any time from 11am to 2pm depending on the number of naps and what we've been up to in the morning. If your child doesn't eat breakfast until 9am then trying lunch at 11am isn't going to be a great success; they probably won't be hungry. Stagger your meals to roughly four hours apart so your baby's stomach has time to empty before you offer more food. Mealtimes are much more likely to be successful if they're offered on an empty tummy and eaten in company. You may find your child showing more interest in food at lunchtime so offering a dinner dish then with a lighter bite in the evening might prove a more successful combination.

## Broccoli and Cheese Muffins (P/LB)

Preparation Time: 20 minutes
Cooking Time: 15 minutes
**Makes 6–8 muffins**

### Ingredients

1 small head of broccoli
1 tub (360ml) full-fat natural yoghurt
1 egg
2 handfuls of grated cheese
200g self-raising flour
Full-fat milk
Butter for greasing
Glug of olive oil
Optional: grated courgette, red onion, spring onion, grated carrot, spinach

### Method

1. Preheat the oven to 200C/180C fan/gas 4
2. Boil or steam the broccoli for around 10 minutes or until tender
3. Meanwhile, in a food processor, blitz the yoghurt, oil and egg
4. Add the broccoli and cheese and pulse in short bursts
5. Add the flour and pulse again. It should look pretty lumpy and unappetizing at this point but that's perfect. Add more flour to thicken and a splash of milk to thin
6. Stir in any optional ingredients you have
7. Freeze the mixture at this point if doing so
8. Grease the muffin tin or baking tray
9. Spoon the mixture into the muffin tin or onto the baking tray to make patties
10. Bake for 15 minutes or until golden brown. You will know they are cooked when you pierce with a knife and it comes out clean

> *Tip*: These make great snacks and are perfect for picnics.

# Omelette Crêpes (P/LB)

Preparation Time: 10 minutes
Cooking Time: 15 minutes
**Serves 1 little person**

## Ingredients

Leftover Drop Scone batter (page 42)
2 eggs
Full-fat milk
1tbsp unsalted butter
¼ onion
¼ red or yellow pepper
1 handful of grated cheese

## Method

1. Stir a splash of milk into the leftover batter to make it a little runnier
2. Melt ½tbsp of butter in a frying pan on a medium heat
3. Add a spoonful of batter and roll around to coat the base of the pan in a thin layer
4. Once brown, use a spatula to flip over, brown the other side and set aside
5. Freeze any crêpes at this point if doing so
6. Chop the onion and peppers and fry in the remaining butter for 5 minutes until soft
7. Whisk the eggs in a bowl and tip over the onion and peppers. Lift and fold the mixture with a spatula so the entire mixture stiffens and cooks through
8. Remove from heat and sprinkle with the cheese. Pop a lid on and leave to stand for 5 minutes until the cheese melts
9. Spoon the mixture into a crepe and roll into a sausage shape

---

*Tip*: Experiment with fillings. Ideal for using up any leftover veggies, such as wilted spinach or grated carrot.

*Tip*: This recipe may take a bit of practice to get the consistency right. Add more plain flour to thicken the batter and milk to thin.

*Adult add-on*: Turn into a dessert of Apple and Calvados Crêpes: Grate 1 large eating apple (Granny Smiths are ideal) and soak with Calvados brandy with a pinch of cinnamon and add to the batter mixture. Cook the pancakes following steps 1–4. Whisk 2tbsp of Calvados with some double cream and serve.

*Leftovers*: The crêpes are ideal for the freezer and can be pulled out for serving with Banana Ice Cream (page 181), Fruit Compote (page 35) and Fruit Purée (page 36) for a yummy dessert or breakfast.

## Sandwiches (P/LB)

Preparation Time: 5 minutes
**Serves 1 little person**

### Ingredients

1 slice of Bread (page 39)
Unsalted butter (optional)
Filling of your choice, such as: full-fat soft cheese with any of the following: avocado,
    grated cucumber, chopped tomato, tinned tuna, tinned salmon, Guacamole
    (page 140); grated Cheddar cheese with grated cucumber or tomato, hummus,
    Hard Boiled Eggs (page 69) or Scrambled Egg (page 40)

### Method

1.   Cut the sandwich into fingers or triangles for your baby to chew on

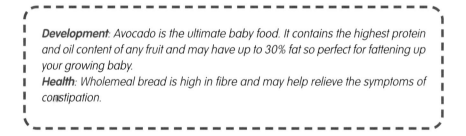

*Development: Avocado is the ultimate baby food. It contains the highest protein and oil content of any fruit and may have up to 30% fat so perfect for fattening up your growing baby.*
*Health: Wholemeal bread is high in fibre and may help relieve the symptoms of constipation.*

# Toasted Cheesy Pitta Pockets (P/LB)

Preparation Time: 5 minutes
Cooking Time: 5 minutes
**Serves 1 little person**

## Ingredients

1 pitta bread
2 thin slices of Cheddar cheese
½ tomato (chopped)

## Method

1.  Preheat the grill
2.  Cut the pitta in half width-ways to make two pockets
3.  Slide a slice of cheese and some tomato into each pocket
4.  Pop under the grill for a couple of minutes until the cheese has melted

*Tip: The cheese may take a while to cool so check before serving.*
***Development**: Cheese is high in vitamin B12 and calcium. Vitamin B12 is more commonly found in meat, making cheese an ideal food for vegetarian babies.*
***Health**: The milk protein responsible for many dairy allergies is largely broken down as it matures so your dairy-sensitive baby may be able to tolerate cheese.*

## Pitta Pizza (P/LB)

Preparation Time: 15 minutes
Cooking Time: 20 minutes
**Serves 1 little person**

### Ingredients

1 pitta bread
Squidge of tomato purée or passata
Handful of grated cheese
Pinch of oregano (optional)

### Method

1. Preheat the oven to 200C/180C fan/gas 6
2. Spread a thin layer of tomato purée or passata over the pitta bread
3. Sprinkle with grated cheese and oregano
4. Bake in the oven for 20 minutes or until the cheese has melted
   This is a basic margarita recipe but our Pizza Base recipe (page 122) offers some more ideas for pizza toppings

*Health: Oregano is a great natural antibiotic so may help with coughs and colds.*

# Fish Fingers (P/LB)

Preparation Time: 15 minutes
Cooking Time: 20 minutes
**Serves 1 little person**

## Ingredients

1 fillet of white fish (boned and skinned) – coley, sole, plaice, salmon and cod are ideal
2 eggs
3tbsp plain flour
2 slices of oldish Bread (page 39)

## Method

1. Preheat the oven to 200C/180C fan/gas 6
2. Tip the flour into a small bowl and set aside
3. Whisk the eggs in a separate bowl and set aside
4. Blitz the bread in a food processor to make breadcrumbs. Alternatively, pop in a freezer bag, cover with a tea towel and beat into crumbs with a rolling pin
5. Tip the breadcrumbs into a third bowl and set aside
6. Cut the fish into strips or shapes of your choice
7. Dip the fish in the flour then the egg and finally the breadcrumbs
8. Spread the fish fingers out on a baking tray and pop in the oven for around 20 minutes or until golden and cooked through

If you prefer, these can be pan-fried by melting 1tsp butter in a frying pan and cooking over a medium heat.

---

*Tip*: It may be less expensive to use frozen fish that is already skinned and boned. Defrost thoroughly before use. See page 218 for information on defrosting foods.
*Tip*: For an extra twist, try adding grated Parmesan cheese to the breadcrumbs.
**Adult add-on**: Fish finger sandwiches are yummy. Serve in a burger bun with a handful of rocket, lemon wedges and tartar sauce on the side.
**Leftovers**: You can freeze any uncooked leftovers (as long as the fish hasn't been frozen previously) but if you've leftover cooked Fish Fingers try the Fish Cakes recipe (page 154).
**Development**: Fish contains omega-3, which may help your baby's immune system to fight off infections.

# Turkey Burgers (P/LB)

Preparation Time: 10 minutes
Cooking Time: 20 minutes
**Serves 2 grown-ups and 1 little person**

## Ingredients

400g turkey mince
1 apple or pear (grated or blitzed
  in a food processor)
½tsp cinnamon
½tsp garlic (crushed)
1tsp unsalted butter

## Method

1. Preheat oven to 200C/180C fan/gas 6
2. Grease a baking tray with the butter
3. Mix the remaining ingredients in a bowl
4. Shape the mixture into patties and lay on the baking tray
5. Oven bake for 20 minutes or until well browned

*Tip*: These can also be pan-fried: melt a dollop of butter in a frying pan over a medium heat and fry for approximately 10 minutes, turning regularly.
*Tip*: This is a great recipe to add leftover vegetables to, such as chopped spinach, grated carrot or frozen peas.
*Tip*: You can also use lean minced beef, lamb or pork instead of turkey mince.
***Leftovers***: If not cooking all the mixture, try the Turkey Meatloaf recipe (page 57).

# Turkey Meatloaf (P/LB)

Preparation Time: 10 minutes
Cooking Time: 20 minutes
**Serves 1 grown-up and 1 little person**

## Ingredients

Leftover Turkey Burger mix (page 56)
Handful of porridge oats
1 egg
1 onion (chopped)
1tbsp unsalted butter

## Method

1. Preheat oven to 200C/180 fan/gas 6
2. Melt ½tbsp of butter in a pan and fry the onion until soft
3. Stir the remaining ingredients into the pan with the onion and fry for a few minutes
4. Grease a loaf tin with ½tbsp butter.
5. Tip the mixture in and press down into the tin
6. Oven bake for 20 minutes or until well browned

*Tip*: This is a great recipe to add leftover vegetables to, such as chopped spinach, grated carrot or frozen peas.
**Leftovers**: Cut any leftovers into large chunks and serve cold on a picnic.
**Development**: The B vitamins in turkey are useful in supporting your baby's rapidly developing nervous system.

# Chicken and Apple Sausages (P/LB)

Preparation Time: 10 minutes
Cooking Time: 20 minutes
**Serves 1 grown-up and 1 little person**

## Ingredients

2 chicken breasts/skinless and boneless
    chicken thigh fillets/turkey steaks
2 carrots
2 apples
2 slices of oldish Bread (page 39)
1 egg
1tsp unsalted butter

## Method

1. Blitz the bread in a food processor to make breadcrumbs. Alternatively, pop in a freezer bag, cover with a tea towel and beat with a rolling pin until required texture is achieved and tip into a separate bowl
2. Whisk the egg in a bowl and set aside
3. Blitz the chicken, carrots and apples in a food processor to make a gooey sludge
4. Shape the chicken mixture into sausages or nuggets of your choosing
5. Dip the chicken pieces in the egg, then the breadcrumbs. If freezing, do so at this point
6. Melt the butter in a frying pan on a medium heat
7. Shallow fry in the pan until golden. These can also be oven baked on a greased baking tray at 200C/180C fan/gas 6 for 20 minutes.

> **Development**: Carrots contain beta-carotene, which is converted to vitamin A, helping your child's developing eyesight.

# Filo Fingers (P/LB)

Preparation Time: 15 minutes
Cooking Time: 15 minutes
**Serves 1 little person**

## Ingredients

2 sheets of ready-made filo pastry
1 egg
Fillings: grated cheese, cream cheese, tinned tuna, chopped tomato

## Method

1. Preheat the oven as directed on the pastry packet
2. Whisk the egg in a cup and set aside
3. Lay 1 filo sheet out and brush with some egg to make it sticky
4. Lay the other filo sheet over the top to give strength
5. Cut the sheets into quarter squares – each will be a finger
6. Spoon a little filling onto each quarter and roll into a sausage shape
7. Place the fingers on a greased baking tray and brush with more egg
8. Pop in the oven for around 15 minutes or until the fingers are brown

---

*Adult add-on*: Try filling with wilted spinach and crumbled Stilton and tie into small parcels with chives for a lovely starter or canapé.
*Leftovers*: These make lovely snacks served cold and are perfect for a picnic.

# Cheese Pastry Bites (P/LB)

Preparation Time: 10 minutes
Cooking Time: 20 minutes
**Serves 2 grown-ups and 1 little person**

## Ingredients

½ pack puff pastry
Sliced Cheddar cheese
1 egg
1tsp unsalted butter
1tsp plain flour

## Method

1. Preheat the oven to 200C/180C fan/gas 6
2. Roll the pastry out thinly on a lightly floured surface and cut into thick strips
3. Place a slice of cheese near the top of the strip and fold and roll over the rest, pressing down to seal
4. If freezing, do so at this point
5. Whisk the egg in a small bowl and brush to coat the pastry bite
6. Place on a greased baking tray and pop into the oven for about 20 minutes or until golden

*Leftovers*: Use up any leftover pastry with the Cheese and Tomato Tartlet (page 61)

# Cheese and Tomato Tartlet (P/LB)

Preparation Time: 15 minutes
Cooking Time: 20 minutes
**Serves 1 adult and 1 little person**

## Ingredients

½ pack puff pastry
1 tin chopped tomatoes
Cheddar cheese (sliced or grated)
Cherry tomatoes (sliced)
1 egg
1tsp unsalted butter
1tsp plain flour

## Method

1. Preheat the oven to 200C/180C fan/gas 6
2. Roll the pastry out thinly on a lightly floured surface and cut into portion sizes and shapes of your choice
3. Place the pastry tartlets on a greased baking tray
3. Spread on the chopped tomatoes, stopping around 1cm from the perimeter
4. Arrange the fresh tomatoes and scatter with the cheese
5. Brush the edges of the tartlets with the beaten egg
5. Bake in the oven for 15–20 minutes or until the pastry edges are golden brown and risen

*Adult add-on*: Roll out the pastry as a single, large, flat rectangular base; Swap Cheddar for mozzarella and add some ham. Before serving, scatter with fresh rocket for an eye-pleasing buffet lunch.

# Chicken Fingers (P/LB)

Preparation Time: 10 minutes
Cooking Time: 15 minutes
**Serves 1 little person**

## Ingredients

1 chicken breast or skinless and boneless chicken thigh fillet
1 egg
Plain flour for dipping
2 slices of oldish Bread (page 39)
1tbsp unsalted butter or oil

## Method

1. Blitz the bread in a food processor to make breadcrumbs. Alternatively, pop in a freezer bag, cover with a tea towel and beat into crumbs with a rolling pin. Tip the breadcrumbs into a bowl and set aside
2. Whisk the egg in a different bowl and set aside
3. Tip the flour into a separate bowl and set aside
4. Cut the chicken into strips and dip in the flour, egg and finally the breadcrumbs
5. Melt the butter or oil in a frying pan
6. Fry until golden on both sides

*Health*: Chicken contains zinc, which may help with symptoms of glue ear.

# Chicken Liver Pâté (P/LB)

Preparation Time: 5 minutes
Cooking Time: 10 minutes
**Serves 2 grown-ups and 1 litte person**

## Ingredients
250g packet of chicken livers (organic preferably)
1tbsp unsalted butter

**TO SERVE:** Toast (page 38); Oatcakes (page 202); Oatcake Biscuits (page 203)

## Method
1. Melt the butter and fry the livers for around 5 minutes or until the liver hardens
2. Pop in a food blender or mash with a fork

*Tip*: Frozen chicken livers may be less expensive to buy than fresh.
*Tip*: Organic chicken livers may be better suited for your child. The liver is the factory of the body, processing food and absorbing any toxins to which the chicken may have been exposed.
**Adult add-on**: Liven this dish up for a grown-up starter by adding to the blender: 50ml double cream, 1tbsp brandy and a pinch of salt and pepper. Pop into ramekins, cover and chill in the fridge. Serve with hot toast and spicy chutney.
**Health**: Chicken livers contain more vitamins, minerals and essential nutrients, gram for gram, than any other food.

# Watercress and Spinach Pâté (P/LB)

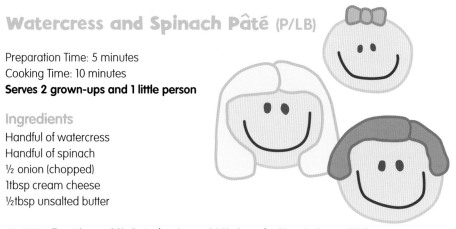

Preparation Time: 5 minutes
Cooking Time: 10 minutes
**Serves 2 grown-ups and 1 little person**

## Ingredients
Handful of watercress
Handful of spinach
½ onion (chopped)
1tbsp cream cheese
½tbsp unsalted butter

**TO SERVE:** Toast (page 38); Oatcakes (page 202); Oatcake Biscuits (page 203)

## Method
1. Fry the onion in the butter until softened
2. Add the watercress and spinach and cook until they wilt
3. Stir in the cream cheese
3. Pop the mixture in a food blender, or mash with a fork

> *Tip*: Growing watercress is an easy and fun activity for your children. Pop to the garden centre, buy a pack of seeds and follow the instructions.
> *Leftovers*: Blend any leftover watercress into a Watercress, Pear and Melon Smoothie (page 188).
> *Leftovers*: Use any leftovers as a yummy filling for a baked potato.
> *Development*: Watercress contains a high level of calcium – more than an average glass of milk and will help with your baby's developing bones and teeth.
> *Health*: Watercress is a super-food. Gram for gram it contains more vitamin C than oranges, more iron than spinach and more calcium than milk.

# Pea and Mint Soup

Preparation Time: 5 minutes
Cooking Time: 25 minutes
**Serves 1 grown-up and 1 little person**

## Ingredients

1 bunch of spring onions (chopped)
1 potato (peeled and chopped)
1 garlic clove (crushed)
500ml Vegetable or Chicken Stock (page 116)
250g frozen peas
4tbsp chopped fresh mint (or 2tbsp dried mint)

## Method

1.  Put the spring onions, potato, garlic and stock in a pan and boil for 20 minutes or until the potato is soft
2.  Add the peas and mint and cook for 5 minutes
3.  Pour into a food processor and whizz until as smooth as you like (it will thicken as it cools)

> **Tip**: Make this thick and gloopy and serve with chunky Bread (page 39) to act as a spoon.
> **Health**: Mint can calm an upset stomach and help improve the respiratory system.

# Leek and Potato Soup

Preparation Time: 15 minutes
Cooking Time: 30 minutes
**Serves 2 grown-ups and 2 little people**

## Ingredients

½tbsp unsalted butter
1 onion (chopped)
3 medium leeks (chopped)
2 potatoes (peeled and thinly sliced)
500ml Chicken Stock (page 116)
Splash of full-fat milk
Black pepper to season

**TO SERVE:** crusty Bread (page 39)

## Method

1. Heat the butter in a pan and cook the onions and leeks slowly on a low heat
2. Add the potatoes, stock and season with black pepper
3. Bring to the boil and simmer for 20–30 minutes until the potato is tender
4. Put into a blender and liquidize
5. Before serving add a splash of milk

*Adult add-on: instead of milk add a splash of cream before serving.*

# Kale Omelette

Preparation Time: 25 minutes
Cooking Time: 5 minutes
**Serves 1 little person**

## Ingredients
Handful of kale
1 potato (peeled and sliced)
½ onion (chopped)
2 eggs
Splash of full-fat milk
½tbsp unsalted butter or glug of olive oil

## Method
1. Steam or boil the potatoes for 10–15 minutes until tender
2. Heat the butter or oil in a frying pan; add the onions and kale for 5 minutes until softened
3. Add the potatoes
4. Whisk the eggs and milk together and pour into the pan
5. Cook for 5 minutes until the mixture firms up. Using a spatula, flip over and cook the other side

*Tip*: This is a great recipe for using up kale that might be going a bit soggy in the fridge.

# Crunchy Kale (P/LB)

Preparation Time: 1–2 minutes
Cooking Time: 1–2 minutes
**Serves 1 little person**

## Ingredients

Handful of kale
1tsp paprika

## Method

1. Preheat the oven to 200C/180C Fan/gas 6
2. Cover a baking tray with foil and scatter the kale across it
3. Sprinkle over the paprika and toss to cover
4. Pop in the oven for 1 or 2 minutes until it starts to brown and crisp up
5. Serve and watch your little one explore the interesting texture

*Tip*: Crunchy Kale makes a great, healthy snack. The unusual texture will be curious and the spiciness of the paprika will enhance their taste buds.
*Leftovers*: Use in Quinoa and Kale Crustless Quiche (page 70) or Kale Omelette (page 67)
*Health*: Kale is one of the healthiest vegetables and can help reduce inflammation that your child might be suffering with if they're teething.

# Hard Boiled Eggs (P/LB)

Cooking Time: 13 minutes
**Serves: variable – 1 egg per little person
and 2 eggs per grown-up**

## Ingredients
Eggs

## Method
1. Place the eggs into a small saucepan and fill with enough cold water to cover them
2. Place on the hob and bring the water to boiling point then turn the heat down and simmer for 7 minutes
3. After the 7 minutes take off the heat and run the cold tap over the eggs immediately for a minute or so (to stop them from being overcooked)
4. Leave them in the cold water for a couple of minutes
5. When cool enough to touch, tap each egg against a hard surface and peel the shell

*Tip*: Hard Boiled Eggs are versatile: slice or chop them for a Sandwich (page 52) filler, quarter them and give them as a snack or drop them into a salad.

# Quinoa and Kale Crustless Quiche (P/LB)

Preparation time: 20 minutes
Cooking time: 45 minutes
**Serves 2 grown-ups and 1 little person**

## Ingredients

125g quinoa
Glug of olive oil
1 bunch/handful of kale (finely chopped)
1 red onion (sliced)
2 cloves of garlic (crushed)
2 handfuls of grated cheese
5tbsp cream cheese or full-fat natural yoghurt
4 eggs
1tsp unsalted butter

## Method

1. Preheat the oven to 180C/160C fan/gas 4
2. Grease a 23cm pie dish (roughly) with the butter
3. Cook the quinoa according to packet instructions and set aside
4. Heat the oil in a large frying pan on medium heat and cook the onion and garlic until soft
5. Remove the onion & garlic and set aside
6. Add the kale to the pan, cooking for 2–3 minutes until wilted
7. Remove the pan from the heat, add the onion, garlic, grated cheese and cream cheese/yoghurt to the kale and mix together
8. Whisk the eggs and tip into the pan, stirring until it all sticks together
9. Pour the mixture in the pie dish and bake for about 45 minutes, until the top is golden brown and the pie has started to pull away from the edge of the baking dish then allow to cool and serve

*Tip*: If you don't have kale, try using spinach instead.
**Adult add-on**: Try using feta cheese instead of the cream cheese for an alternative flavour.

# Shortcrust Pastry

Preparation Time: 10 minutes, plus 30 minutes resting
**Makes 225g pastry**

## Ingredients

225g plain flour
110g unsalted butter
Cold water

## Method

1. Put the flour and butter in a food processor, whizzing until it resembles fine crumbs
2. Add 3–4tbsp cold water and process briefly using the pulse button until the mixture sticks together, forming a ball
3. Put on a floured surface and knead lightly to form a smooth, firm dough then wrap in cling film and leave to rest in the fridge for 30 minutes or until ready to use

---

*Leftovers*: Store any leftover pastry in the freezer or use to make Mini Meaty Pasties (page 162) or Gingerbread People (page 195).

*Leftovers*: Use up leftover pastry by making a Jam Doughnut. Roll out some pastry and then dollop some Fruit Purée (page 36) or Fruit Compote (page 35) in the middle, bringing the edges in to cover. Roll in the palm of your hand to form a small ball and pop on a baking tray in the oven for 10–15 minutes until cooked on 180C/160C fan/gas 4. Be sure it's cooled thoroughly before eating as the 'jam' gets very hot.

*Leftovers*: Make Jam Tarts by rolling out the pastry thinly and cutting out circles using pastry cutters of your choice. Place them into a greased shallow bun or muffin tin. Prick the pastry then add a dollop of jam into the middle and bake in the oven on 180C/160C fan/gas 4 until the pastry turns golden.

---

# Falafels (P/LB)

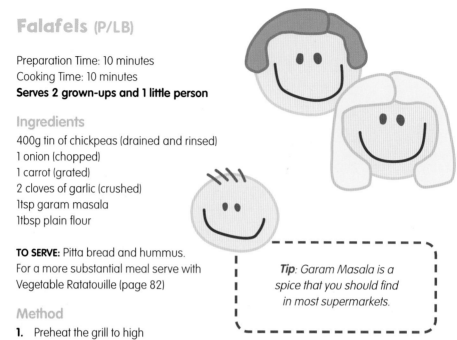

Preparation Time: 10 minutes
Cooking Time: 10 minutes
**Serves 2 grown-ups and 1 little person**

## Ingredients

400g tin of chickpeas (drained and rinsed)
1 onion (chopped)
1 carrot (grated)
2 cloves of garlic (crushed)
1tsp garam masala
1tbsp plain flour

**TO SERVE:** Pitta bread and hummus.
For a more substantial meal serve with
Vegetable Ratatouille (page 82)

*Tip: Garam Masala is a spice that you should find in most supermarkets.*

## Method

1. Preheat the grill to high
2. Tip the chickpeas, onion, carrot, garlic
   and garam masala into a food processor and blend into a chunky texture
3. Stir in the flour
4. Take spoonfuls of the mixture and shape into patties, placing on a grill pan lined with foil
5. Brush the tops with oil and then grill for 5 minutes
6. Once golden turn the patties over, oil again and grill for a further 5 minutes

Chapter Six

# Dinner

Try to avoid offering too much fruit at the evening meal. Fruit is a carbohydrate so won't fill your baby up for as long as a high protein meal. Fruit in the evenings may also lead to a soiled nappy in the middle of the night, again because it will be digested much quicker than proteins or fats.

There is, of course, no reason why you can't use the lunch recipes for dinner time, but these recipes are designed with the family meal in mind.

Some recipes may include wine as an optional *adult add-on* ingredient to help enhance their flavour. Incidentally, when the dishes are cooked long enough, usually several minutes, the alcohol will evaporate leaving only harmless trace residues.

# Fish Pie

Preparation Time: 40 minutes
Cooking Time: 30 minutes
**Serves 2 grown-ups and 2 little ones**

## Ingredients

2 salmon fillets (boneless)
2 white fish fillets (boneless): coley, sole, plaice and cod are all ideal
4 baking potatoes (peeled and halved)
1 onion (chopped)

2 handfuls of cheese (grated or crumbled into small chunks)
3tbsp flour
100ml full-fat milk
1tsp unsalted butter
Handful of frozen peas (optional)

## Method

1. Preheat the oven to 180C/160C fan/gas 4
2. Peel the potatoes and steam or boil for 40 minutes until soft for mashing
3. Melt the butter in a large pan over a medium heat, add the onion and cook for 5 minutes until softened
4. Cut the fish into chunks and coat with flour
5. Add the fish and the cheese to the pan and stir until the cheese melts
6. Add the milk and stir. It will thicken as it cooks over a few minutes. It should be thick and gloopy like wallpaper paste. Add more milk to thin and more flour or cheese to thicken. Add the frozen peas if using
7. Turn off the heat but leave the pan on the cooling hob to continue to cook whilst you mash the potatoes with some butter and a splash of milk
8. Tip the fish mixture into an ovenproof dish and spread over the mashed potato
9. Bake in the oven for 25–30 minutes

*Tip*: Thick and gloopy fish pie is perfect for little ones to pick up with their fingers. As they get older, add more milk to make a sloppier sauce to challenge their spoon and fork control.

*Leftovers*: Make Fish Pie Fritters: sieve the leftover Fish Pie so you're left with a gloopy mixture. Roll in some breadcrumbs and fry in butter or oil until brown all over. Serve with some rocket and Salsa (page 139) for a yummy lunch.

*Development*: Salmon is rich in vitamin E. Recent research suggests developmental disorders such as ADHD (attention deficit hyperactivity disorder) and autism spectrum disorders may be linked to a deficiency of fatty acids such as vitamin E.

# Chilli Bolognese

Preparation Time: 10 minutes
Cooking Time: 40 minutes
**Serves 2 grown-ups and 1 little person**

## Ingredients

Leftover Meaty Bolognese (page 125)
  or Lentil Bolognese (page 124)
1 tin of kidney beans
1tsp chilli powder
1tsp ground cumin
1tsp ground coriander
Optional: tin of chopped tomatoes

**TO SERVE:** pasta; rice; baked potato; quinoa; couscous

## Method

1. Mix all the ingredients together in a saucepan
2. Cook over a medium heat, making sure the meat/lentils are thoroughly heated through. If you need more mixture, add a tin of chopped tomatoes
2. Adjust seasoning according to your taste

*Development: Kidney beans contain vitamin B1 (thiamine), which helps produce energy so your little one can lead an active life.*
*Health: Chilli may help reduce inflammation, soothing your baby's symptoms from conjunctivitis or teething.*

# Pizza Bolognese

Preparation Time: 5 minutes
Cooking Time: 15 minutes
**Makes 1 pizza**

## Ingredients
Leftover Meaty Bolognese (page 125) or Lentil Bolognese (page 124)
Pizza Base (page 122)
Handful of grated cheese

## Method
1. Preheat the oven to 200C/180C fan/gas 6
2. Spread the Bolognese sauce over the pizza base
3. Place the pizza on a baking sheet, sprinkle with grated cheese and pop in the oven for 10–15 minutes until the cheese has melted and starts to brown

# Pasty Bolognese

Preparation Time: 10 minutes
Cooking Time: 20 minutes
**Makes 4–6 pasties**

## Ingredients

Leftover Meaty Bolognese (page 125), Lentil Bolognese (page 124) or Vegetarian Moussaka (page 79)
½ packet of puff pastry or Shortcrust Pastry (page 71)
1 egg
Optional: grated cheese

## Method

1. Preheat the oven to 200C/180C fan/gas 6
2. Roll out the pastry and cut into circles into whatever size you would like your pasties. A large mug is a good template for finger-food sized pasties
3. Spoon a blob of the bolognese into the middle of the pastry circle, leaving a 1cm gap around the edge. Add some grated cheese if using. Be careful not to overfill otherwise they will burst when cooking
4. Beat the egg and use a pastry brush to brush over the 1cm space
5. Fold the pastry edges together so they meet and use your fingers or a fork to seal shut
6. Brush the outside of the pasties with the egg and pop in the oven for 20 minutes or until the outside is golden

# Vegetarian Moussaka

Preparation Time: 45 minutes
Cooking Time: 45 minutes
**Serves 2 grown-ups and 2 little people**

## Ingredients

Glug of olive oil or 1tsp unsalted butter
1 tin (400g) puy or green lentils (before
   embarking on this recipe, check the
   lentils don't need pre-cooking)
1 onion (chopped)
2 cloves garlic (crushed)
2 carrots (cut into batons)
2 sticks of celery (chopped)

2tsp ground cinnamon
   or ground mixed spice
1 tin of plum tomatoes
1tbsp of tomato purée
1 aubergine (finely sliced into discs)
250g full-fat natural yoghurt
1 egg
1 handful of grated Cheddar cheese

**TO SERVE:** salad or steamed vegetables

## Method

1. Steam or boil the carrots for 20 minutes to soften
3. Melt the butter or olive oil in a pan, adding the onions and garlic
4. Once the onions have softened, add the carrots, celery, cinnamon or mixed spice, and gently fry for 5 minutes
5. Add the lentils and tomatoes and leave to simmer for 20 minutes
6. Add the tomato purée and leave to cook for another 10 minutes until the sauce is sludgy
7. In a lasagne dish, add a layer of aubergine, then sauce, and repeat until all the aubergine and sauce is used, finishing with a layer of aubergine
8. Mix together the yoghurt, egg and two thirds of the grated cheese and pour on top of the aubergine
9. Sprinkle with the remaining grated cheese and pop it in the oven for 45 minutes or until a knife goes easily through the aubergine

*Tip*: The smaller the aubergine you choose the less bitter and more tender it will be.
**Adult add-on**: A slosh (50–100ml) of red wine added in with the lentils and tomatoes at stage 4 will bring out the flavour of the dish.
**Leftovers**: Use any remaining aubergine in Vegetable Ratatouille (page 82).
**Leftovers**: Spread leftover moussaka on a Pizza Base (page 122) or mix in with Pasty Bolognese (page 78).
**Health**: Aubergine is high in fibre, and will help keep your baby's stools soft and regular.

## Moroccan Stew

Preparation Time: 20 minutes
Cooking Time: 2 hours
**Serves 2 grown-ups and 2 little people**

### Ingredients

Glug of olive oil or 1tsp unsalted butter
1 onion (chopped)
2 cloves of garlic (crushed)
½ butternut squash (peeled and cut into chunks)
4 carrots (peeled and chopped into batons)
2 tins chopped tomatoes
450ml Vegetable or Chicken Stock (page 116)
1tsp ground cumin
½tsp ground cinnamon
400g tin of chickpeas (drained and rinsed)
Handful of sage leaves (chopped)

**TO SERVE:** pasta; rice; couscous; quinoa; baked potato

## Method

1. Heat the oil in a large saucepan
2. Add the onion and garlic and cook until softened
3. Add butternut squash, carrots, tomatoes, stock, cumin, cinnamon and chickpeas
4. Cover and simmer on a low heat for 2 hours. Alternatively, if you have a slow cooker pop on medium for 6 hours or until the squash is soft and squidgy

*Tip*: It can be quicker to buy tins of pre-cooked chickpeas but these are often more expensive than dried chickpeas, which will need soaking and pre-cooking. Check the packet for instructions.

*Tip*: When choosing a butternut squash, opt for a long skinny one if you can. The seeds are in the base of the squash so there's less time spent removing them.

*Development*: Sage is a really easy herb to grow in the garden and may help improve memory.

*Health*: Garlic may help fight off colds and infections.

*Health*: Butternut squash provides anti-inflammatory benefits, which may help reduce the symptoms of teething, conjunctivitis or ear infections.

# Vegetable Ratatouille

Preparation Time: 10 minutes
Cooking Time: 50 minutes
**Serves 2 grown-ups and 2 little people**

## Ingredients

1tsp butter or glug of olive oil
1 aubergine (diced)
1 onion (chopped)
2 cloves garlic (crushed)
500ml of Vegetable Stock (page 116)
1 tin of chopped tomatoes
Squidge of tomato purée
1 pepper (chopped)
Handful of spinach (chopped)
6 mushrooms (chopped)

**TO SERVE:** pasta; rice; couscous; quinoa; baked potato

## Method

1. Heat the oil or butter in a large saucepan. Add the onion and garlic, frying until soft. Add the aubergine and cook until soft
2. Pour in the stock and bring to the boil, simmering on a low heat until the liquid has almost gone
3. Add the chopped tomatoes, tomato purée, pepper and mushrooms and simmer for around 5 minutes
4. Just before serving add the spinach and stir through

*Development: Spinach helps red cell production. Red blood cells carry the oxygen throughout your little one, giving them energy.*

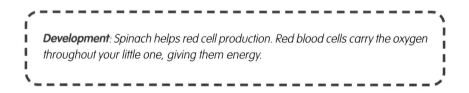

# Seafood Risotto

Preparation Time: 10 minutes
Cooking Time: 45 minutes
**Serves 2 grown-ups
  and 2 little people**

## Ingredients

1 onion (chopped)
2 cloves garlic (crushed)
200g mixed frozen seafood
150g uncooked rice
1tsp unsalted butter
Handful of frozen peas
285ml Vegetable or Chicken Stock (page 116)

## Method

1.  Cook the rice according to the packet instructions
2.  Meanwhile, melt the butter in a large saucepan
3.  Add the garlic and onion and fry until the onion softens
4.  Add the stock, seafood and peas and simmer for 30 minutes
5.  Once cooked, mix together the rice and seafood and serve

---

*Tip*: If using risotto rice, melt a knob of butter in a pan over a medium heat and cook the onion and garlic until soft. Add the risotto rice and stir until it is coated in the butter. Add the stock a little at a time, until the rice absorbs the liquid. Repeat until approximately half the stock has gone. Add the seafood and peas and resume adding the stock until all the stock has gone and the liquid has been absorbed in the pan.

*Adult add-on*: Once the onion has softened, add a slosh of white wine and leave to simmer for a couple of minutes.

*Adult add-on*: Stir through a squeeze of lemon juice and a sprinkle of Parmesan to finish.

*Leftovers*: Make Arancini di Riso (page 84).

*Development*: Seafood helps support your child's rapidly developing brain, eyes and nerves.

*Health*: Rice may help firm up your baby's stools if they have diarrhoea.

*Warning*: Avoid serving shellfish to babies less than 12 months old.

# Arancini di Riso

Preparation Time: 10 minutes
Cooking Time: 20 minutes
**Serves 1 grown-up and 1 little person**

## Ingredients

Leftover Seafood Risotto (page 83)
1tsp unsalted butter or 1 glug of olive oil
1 egg
2 slices of oldish Bread (page 39)
Optional: mozzarella

## Method

1. Crack the egg into the risotto and mix together to make a gloopy mixture
2. Make some breadcrumbs by blitzing the bread in a food processor. Alternatively, pop in a freezer bag, cover with a tea towel and beat into crumbs with a rolling pin and set aside
3. Roll the risotto mixture into small balls, inserting an optional small cube of mozzarella in the centre of each
4. Roll the ball in breadcrumbs to coat
5. Melt the butter or oil in a frying pan
6. Place the rice balls in the pan and cook for around 5 minutes until golden brown and heated through, turning as necessary
7. Transfer to paper towel to drain

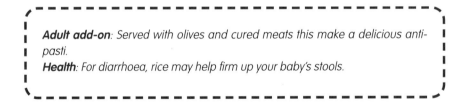

*Adult add-on*: Served with olives and cured meats this make a delicious anti-pasti.
*Health*: For diarrhoea, rice may help firm up your baby's stools.

# Frittata (P/LB)

Preparation Time: 5 minutes
Cooking Time: 20 minutes
**Makes 1 Frittata**

## Ingredients

3 eggs
Handful of spinach
Handful of grated cheese
2 tomatoes (finely chopped)
½tbsp unsalted butter
Optional: onion, pepper, peas, leek, diced cooked chicken

**TO SERVE:** salad; steamed vegetables

## Method

1. Whisk the eggs in a bowl and add the cheese, tomatoes and spinach
2. Melt the butter in a frying pan over a medium heat
3. Add the egg mixture, tilting the pan so as to cover the entire base and leave for a few seconds to start firming up
4. Using a spatula, draw the edge of the mixture from the sides to the centre of the pan, allowing the liquid egg to flow into the space created
5. Repeat this continuously until there is no liquid egg left on the surface
6. Fold the frittata in half and serve

> **Tip**: The frittata will continue to cook once removed from the heat.
> **Leftovers**: If you have any leftover egg whites from other recipes, this is an ideal recipe for using them up.

# Cottage Pie

Preparation Time: 35 minutes
Cooking Time: 30 minutes
**Serves 4 grown-ups and 2 little people**

## Ingredients

1tbsp unsalted butter or a glug of olive oil
Splash of full-fat milk
500g minced lamb or beef
4 baking potatoes (peeled and chopped)
1 onion (chopped)
2 cloves of garlic (crushed)
450ml Beef Stock (page 116)
Squidge of tomato purée
Handful of frozen peas
1 large carrot, diced
1 bay leaf

**TO SERVE:** seasonal steamed vegetables

## Method

1. Boil or steam the potatoes for around 30 minutes
2. Preheat the oven to 180C/160C fan/gas 4
3. Fry the onions, garlic and carrot in oil or ½tbsp butter until softened
4. Add the mince and cook until browned
5. Pour over the stock and add the bay leaf, tomato purée and peas
6. Cover and leave to simmer on a low heat for about 15 minutes
7. Once cooked, pour into an ovenproof dish
8. Drain and mash the potatoes with ½tbsp butter and a splash of milk
9. Spread the mashed potato over the mince and bake in the oven for 30 minutes

*Adult add-on*: At the end of step 3 add a slosh of red wine and a splash of Worcester sauce. Simmer for 5 minutes to burn off the alcohol and enhance the flavour.

# Cauliflower and/or Broccoli Cheese

Preparation Time: 15 minutes
Cooking Time: 15 minutes
**Serves 2 adults and 1 little person**

## Ingredients

1 broccoli head and/or
  1 cauliflower head
4 handfuls of grated cheese
1tbsp unsalted butter
1tbsp flour
285ml full-fat milk

## Method

1. Wash and cut/tear the broccoli and/or cauliflower into small florets
2. Steam or boil for about 10 minutes and then put in an ovenproof dish
3. On a low heat melt the butter in a pan then add the flour and stir into a paste
4. Add the milk gradually whilst whisking and turn up the heat slightly; if you add it too quickly you will get lumpy sauce. Keep adding until all the milk is used
5. Add 3 handfuls of grated cheese and keep stirring
6. When the mixture boils pour over the cooked vegetables
7. Cover with the last handful of grated cheese and pop under the grill for 5 minutes or until the top is starting to brown

---

*Tip*: This dish is tasty as a meal in itself or as an accompaniment to cooked fish.
*Tip*: If you don't like cauliflower then simply substitute for more broccoli or vice versa.
*Tip*: If serving this recipe as a main dish, increase the volumes to 2 large broccoli heads and/or 1 large cauliflower, 6 handfuls of grated cheese, 2tbsp unsalted butter, 2tbsp flour, 570ml full-fat milk.
*Adult add-on*: Add cayenne pepper and 1tsp of English mustard when you add the grated cheese to the milk, for a more flavoursome sauce.
*Health*: Broccoli is high in flavonoids, which may help speed up the healing of a bruise.

# Salmon and Broccoli Pasta Bake

Preparation Time: 30 minutes
Cooking Time: 20 minutes
**Serves 2 grown-ups and 1 little person**

## Ingredients

2 skinless and boneless salmon fillets
1 broccoli head
4 handfuls of grated cheese
1tbsp flour
1tbsp unsalted butter
285ml full-fat milk
2tbsp cream cheese (with garlic and herbs can be nice)
Handful of cherry tomatoes (chopped)
150g dried pasta

## Method

1. Cook the salmon either in the steamer for 15 minutes or wrap in foil and bake in the oven on 180C/160C fan/gas 4 for 20 minutes
2. Cut/tear the broccoli into small florets and steam or boil for 10 minutes
3. Cook the pasta as per instructions on the packet, drain and place in an ovenproof dish
4. On a low heat melt the butter in a saucepan, then add the flour and stir into a paste
5. Add the milk gradually whilst whisking and turn up the heat slightly until all the milk is used. If you add the milk too quickly you will get lumpy sauce.
6. Stir in the grated cheese and cream cheese
7. Break the cooked salmon into chunks and add to the pasta
8. Stir in the tomatoes and broccoli and mix well
9. Pour the cheese sauce over the pasta and bake in the oven for 20 minutes

> **Tip**: Try a microwave steamer to quickly steam the fish.
> **Health**: Fish is high in omega-3 fatty acids, which may reduce inflammation in conditions such as conjunctivitis.

# Chicken/Turkey Mornay

Preparation Time: 20 minutes
Cooking Time: 30 minutes
**Serves 2 grown-ups and 2 little people**

## Ingredients

1tbsp unsalted butter or olive oil
4 chicken or turkey breasts (diced)
1 onion (chopped)
½ leek (thinly sliced)
5 celery sticks (thinly sliced)
Tinned carrots (or 2 large fresh carrots, diced and cooked until soft)
2 handfuls of grated cheese
Splash of full-fat milk
1tbsp flour

**TO SERVE:** rice; baked potato; couscous

## Method

1. Preheat the oven to 180C/160C fan/gas 4
2. Heat the oil or butter in a large pan and fry the onion, celery and leek until soft
3. Add the chicken or turkey and carrots and cook until the meat is browned
4. Sprinkle the flour over the ingredients and stir through
5. Add milk and keep stirring until you get a wet sauce
6. Stir in half of the grated cheese
7. At this point the sauce should become a paste-like consistency. However, if the sauce is too thick add more milk, if too thin add more cheese or flour
8. Tip into an ovenproof dish, sprinkle with the remaining cheese and bake in the oven for about 20–30 minutes

*Tip*: This recipe is great for using up leftover Christmas turkey or the Sunday roast chicken.

*Tip*: Try skinless and boneless chicken thigh fillets for a less expensive alternative to chicken breast.

*Adult add-on*: When you add the chicken at step 3, add a few splashes of Worcester sauce.

# Easy-Cheesy Pasta

Preparation Time: 5 minutes
Cooking Time: 15 minutes
**Serves 1 grown-up and 1 little person**

## Ingredients

4 handfuls of dried or fresh pasta
Handful of frozen peas
Handful of frozen sweetcorn
Handful of grated Cheddar cheese
Optional: leftover Yummy Yoghurt-Cheese (page 183)

## Method

1. Cook the pasta according to the instructions on the packet. Just before it's cooked, add the peas and sweetcorn to the water. Drain and set aside
2. Tip the Yoghurt-Cheese (if using) and grated cheese into the pan and cook over a medium heat until the cheese has melted
3. Stir in the pasta, peas and sweetcorn and serve

*Leftovers*: Make a quick *Easy-Cheesy Pasta Bake* by tipping any leftovers into an ovenproof dish. Stir in a tin of tuna (drained) and sprinkle with grated cheese. Pop under the grill for 5–10 minutes until the cheese melts and starts to colour.

# Lamb Stew

Preparation Time: 30 minutes
Cooking Time: 2 hours
**Serves 2 grown-ups and 2 little people**

## Ingredients

1kg lamb, boned and diced
  (e.g. shoulder, leg, shank)
1tbsp olive oil
3 cloves of garlic (crushed)
1 onion (chopped)
1 leek (chopped)
1 red pepper (chopped)
1tsp fresh ginger (grated)
1½tsp ground coriander
1tsp ground cinnamon
2 tins of chopped tomatoes
2tbsp tomato purée
2tbsp honey
Black pepper to season

**TO SERVE:** couscous or Bread (page 39); green beans

## Method

1.  Preheat the oven to 160C/140C fan/gas 4
2.  Heat the olive oil in a saucepan over a low heat and add the onion, garlic, leek, ginger and spices and cook until the onion and leek are soft
3.  Add the lamb, red pepper, tomatoes, tomato purée and honey and season with black pepper. Stir and bring to a simmer
4.  Pour into an ovenproof casserole dish, or tagine, with a lid, and cook in the oven for 1½–2 hours, stirring occasionally. Cook until the lamb is tender
5.  If the sauce is too thin, remove the lid halfway through cooking, to allow the sauce to reduce and thicken

# Meat Balls

Preparation Time: 25 minutes
Cooking Time: 40 minutes
**Serves 2 grown-ups and 2 little people**

## Ingredients

**FOR THE MEATBALLS:**
2 glugs of olive oil
2 cloves of garlic (crushed)
1 onion (finely chopped)
1 green chilli (deseeded and chopped finely)
2tbsp fresh flat leaf parsley
Black pepper to season
500g lean mince beef
1 egg (beaten)

**FOR THE SAUCE:**
1 glug of olive oil
1 onion (chopped)
2 cloves of garlic (chopped)
6 mushrooms (chopped)
1 red pepper (chopped)
1 tin of chopped tomatoes
1tbsp tomato purée
Black pepper to season
Optional: Add courgette or chopped spinach to the sauce

**TO SERVE:** spaghetti or pasta

## Method

1. To make the sauce, heat a glug of olive oil in a frying pan and add the chopped garlic and onion and cook until softened. Add the tomatoes, tomato purée, red pepper and mushrooms, season with black pepper and simmer for about 20 minutes
2. Meanwhile, in another frying pan, heat another glug of oil over a low heat, add the crushed garlic, onion and chilli and cook until the onion is soft. Take off the heat and allow to cool
3. To make the meatballs, tip the mince and onion mixture, parsley and egg into a large bowl and season with black pepper
4. Mash the ingredients with dampened hands and shape the mixture into 12–14 balls
5. Heat another glug of oil in the frying pan and cook the meatballs for about 10 minutes, turning frequently (ensure they are cooked through)
6. Add the meatballs to the sauce and serve.

*Tip*: Freeze any unused chillies. When you come to need one simply take it out of the freezer, chop (deseed if necessary) and then use in your cooking. It's a great way to avoid getting chilli fingers too!

**Adult add-on**: Once you've made enough meatballs for your child add some grated Parmesan to the rest of the mixture.

**Leftovers**: Use any mince mixture leftovers to make home-made beef burgers by simply adding breadcrumbs (or Parmesan cheese for an adult add-on version). Shape into patties and then place under a preheated grill, barbeque or fry them until cooked through.

# Tricolore Pasta

Preparation Time: 15 minutes
Cooking Time: 25 minutes
**Serves 2 grown-ups and 2 little people**

## Ingredients

Glug of olive oil
2 cloves of garlic (chopped)
1 small green chilli (finely chopped)
1 onion (chopped)
1 courgette (diced)
1 red pepper (chopped)
6 mushrooms (diced)
1 tin of chopped tomatoes
1tbsp tomato purée
Black pepper to season
300g dried or fresh pasta
Optional: cooked diced chicken or turkey breast

**TO SERVE:** pasta bows or tagliatelle

## Method

1. Cook the pasta according to the packet instructions, drain and set aside
2. Meanwhile, heat the oil in a pan and add the garlic, chilli and onion and cook until softened. If using, add the diced chicken or turkey at this stage and cook until browned
3. Add the vegetables and cook slowly over a low heat
4. Once the courgette has softened add the tinned tomatoes and tomato purée and season with pepper
5. Stir, bring to a simmer and cook until the sauce reaches your desired consistency

*Adult add-on*: Once the vegetables have cooked put some of them into a separate pan and stir through Pesto (page 117) and pine nuts instead of the tinned tomatoes. Grate some Parmesan cheese over the top to serve.
*Leftovers*: This mix of vegetables with tomatoes is a fantastic topping for a home-made Pizza Base (page 122), simply add grated cheese on top and place in the oven.

# Chicken or Turkey and Broccoli Pasta

Preparation Time: 15 minutes
Cooking Time: 20 minutes
**Serves 2 grown-ups and 2 little people**

## Ingredients

Glug of olive oil
2 cloves of garlic (chopped)
1 onion (chopped)
3 chicken or turkey breasts (diced)
1 small head of broccoli (washed and
  chopped into small florets)
6 mushrooms (diced)
2tbsp Pesto (page 117)
3–4 handfuls dried or fresh pasta

## Method

1. Heat the oil over a low heat and cook the garlic and onions until softened
2. Increase the heat, add the diced chicken or turkey and mushrooms and cook thoroughly
3. Meanwhile, cook the pasta as per the packet instructions and for the last 10 minutes add the broccoli (or steam separately for 10 minutes)
4. Once the pasta and broccoli are cooked, drain and add them to the pan with the vegetables and chicken or turkey, stir in the Pesto and serve

> **Adult add-on**: Sprinkle pine nuts over the dish to serve.

# Tuna Rice

Preparation Time: 10 minutes
Cooking Time: 20 minutes
**Serves 2 grown-ups and 2 little people**

## Ingredients
Glug of olive oil
225g uncooked rice
200g tinned tuna (drained)
2 cloves of garlic (chopped)
1 onion (chopped)
½ red pepper (chopped)
½ courgette (diced)
6 mushrooms (diced)
1 tin of chopped tomatoes
2tbsp tomato purée
Black pepper to season
Fresh parsley

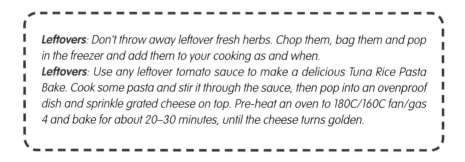

**TO SERVE:** Bread (page 39) and/or broccoli

## Method
1. Cook the rice as per the instructions on the packet; when cooked drain and set aside
2. Meanwhile, heat the oil in a frying pan and cook the garlic and onion until softened
3. Add the rest of the vegetables (apart from the tomatoes) and cook for a further 5 minutes
4. Stir in the tomatoes and tuna and season with black pepper, simmering for 10 minutes
5. Stir in the rice, sprinkle with parsley and serve

---

*Leftovers*: Don't throw away leftover fresh herbs. Chop them, bag them and pop in the freezer and add them to your cooking as and when.
*Leftovers*: Use any leftover tomato sauce to make a delicious Tuna Rice Pasta Bake. Cook some pasta and stir it through the sauce, then pop into an ovenproof dish and sprinkle grated cheese on top. Pre-heat an oven to 180C/160C fan/gas 4 and bake for about 20–30 minutes, until the cheese turns golden.

# Tuna Pasta Bake

Preparation Time: 20 minutes
Cooking Time: 20 minutes
**Serves 3 grown-ups and 2 little people**

## Ingredients

400g dried or fresh pasta
400g tinned tuna (drained)
200g tinned sweetcorn (drained)
1 handful of small broccoli florets
1tbsp unsalted butter
1tbsp plain flour
4 handfuls of grated cheese

## Method

1. Pre-heat the oven to 180C/160C fan/gas 4
2. Cook the pasta as directed on the instructions. For the last 10 minutes add the broccoli florets (or steam the broccoli separately)
3. Meanwhile, make the cheese sauce by heating the butter over a low heat and stir in the flour until you get a paste
4. Turn the heat up slightly and gradually add the milk, whilst stirring all the time to prevent any lumps from forming
5. Just as the sauce begins to boil add 3 handfuls of grated cheese, stir well and remove from the heat
6. Once the pasta and broccoli are cooked, drain and add to the cheese sauce along with the tuna and sweetcorn; stir and place in an ovenproof dish
7. Sprinkle the top with the remaining cheese and bake in the oven for 15–20 minutes, until the cheese turns golden

*Tip*: Instead of using a cheese sauce you could use cream cheese or a tin of tomatoes. Or, replace the tuna with cooked diced chicken and diced mushrooms.
*Adult add-on*: At step 3, stir-in 1tsp of cayenne pepper and 1tsp of English mustard to the cheese sauce.
*Developmental*: Tuna is a nutrient-dense food and an excellent source of protein. Tuna contains omega-3 essential fatty acids, which are essential for the body's health.

# Turkey Tagine

Preparation Time: 40 minutes
Cooking Time: 1½ hours
**Serves 2 grown-ups and 2 little people**

## Ingredients
4 turkey breasts (diced)
Glug of olive oil
1 onion (chopped)
1 leek (chopped)
1 red pepper (chopped)
1 carrot (diced)
2 cloves of garlic (chopped)
1tsp cumin
1tsp cinnamon
1tsp ground ginger (or about a 4cm root of freshly grated ginger)
Black pepper to season
2 tins of chopped tomatoes
1tbsp tomato purée
Handful of dried fruit (chopped apricots, prunes or sultanas)

**TO SERVE:** couscous and green beans or rice

## Method
1.  Pre heat the oven to 160C/140C fan/gas 3
2.  Heat the oil over a low heat and cook the leek and onion until softened
3.  Increase the heat and add the spices, garlic, ginger and turkey and cook until the turkey is browned and cooked through
4.  Add the tomatoes, carrot, pepper, tomato purée and dried fruit, season with black pepper, stir and bring to a simmer
5.  Pour into a tagine or lidded casserole dish and bake in the oven for 1½ hours

# Pasta Gratin

Preparation Time: 10 minutes
Cooking Time: 20 minutes
**Serves 1 grown-up and 1 little person**

## Ingredients
Leftover Spaghetti Carbonara (page 130)
3tbsp unsalted butter
3tbsp plain flour
285ml full-fat milk
1 handful of breadcrumbs
Parmesan cheese and Cheddar cheese (grated)

## Method
1. Preheat the oven to 180C/160C fan/gas 4
2. Melt the butter over a low heat, mix in the flour and continue to stir while slowly adding the milk, stirring continuously to prevent it going lumpy
3. Tip the leftover Spaghetti Carbonara into an ovenproof baking dish and cover with the sauce
4. Mix the cheese and breadcrumbs together and sprinkle over the top
5. Bake in the oven for 15–20 minutes until it is warmed through and the cheese is beginning to melt and turn golden

# Pork Chops

Preparation Time: 10 minutes
Cooking Time: 20 minutes
**Serves 1 grown-up and 1 little person**

## Ingredients
2 pork chops

**FOR THE MARINADE:**
1 squeeze of lemon juice
1 glug of olive oil
1 garlic clove (crushed)
1tsp oregano
1tsp coriander

## Method
1.  Mix the marinade ingredients together and rub into the pork chops. Cover and leave in the fridge for as long as possible, leaving overnight if you can
2.  Heat some oil in a frying pan and fry the chops until cooked or pop under a pre-heated grill for 5–10 minutes

---

*Tip*: The bone of the chop makes an ideal handle for your little one to grasp and they may love having a gnaw on it.
*Adult add-on*: Once you've pan-fried the chops, make a rich sauce by deglazing the pan with a splash of cider, white wine, apple juice, balsamic vinegar, crème fraiche, butter and English mustard. Pour over the chops and serve with mashed potato and spring greens for a hearty supper.

# Eggy Dumplings

Preparation Time: 10 minutes
Cooking Time: 10 minutes
**Serves 1 grown-up and 1 little person**

## Ingredients

Leftover Gnocchi (page 126)
Glug of olive oil
2 eggs

## Method

1. Heat the oil in a frying pan and cook the gnocchi until it starts to turn golden
2. Whisk the eggs together and add to the pan stirring until they are cooked through

# Beany Balls in Tomato Sauce

Preparation Time: 10 minutes
Cooking Time: 30 minutes
**Serves 1 grown-up and 1 little person**

## Ingredients

Leftover uncooked Bean Burger mixture (page 132)
400g chopped fresh tomatoes
1 onion (sliced)
2 garlic cloves (crushed)
1tsp oregano
Glug of olive oil
Ground black pepper

**TO SERVE:** pasta

## Method

1. In a large pan, heat a glug of olive oil, add the onion and garlic and cook until softened
2. Add the tomatoes, season with black pepper and the oregano and cook, uncovered, for 30 minutes or until the tomato softens
4. Meanwhile, shape the bean mixture into small balls
5. In a pan, heat the remaining oil and fry the bean balls until browned all over
6. Once cooked, add the bean balls to the tomato sauce and serve with pasta

# Spicy Baked Chicken with Couscous

Preparation Time: 10 minutes (note: ideally
  the chicken should marinate for a few hours or
  overnight once prepared but this is not essential)
Cooking Time: 30 minutes
**Serves 2 grown-ups and 2 little people**

## Ingredients

500g skinless and boneless chicken thigh fillets
  or 4 chicken breasts
250g couscous
1tbsp medium curry powder
1tbsp paprika
1tsp cinnamon
3 garlic cloves (crushed)
Glug of olive oil
285ml Chicken or Vegetable Stock (page 116)
Handful of sultanas or raisins

## Method

1. Put the chicken in a dish and sprinkle with the curry powder, paprika, cinnamon, garlic
   and olive oil. Rub the mixture into the chicken, cover and leave to marinate in the fridge
   if possible
2. Cook the chicken in the oven (200C/180C fan/gas 6) for 20–30 minutes until the
   chicken is cooked through
3. Put the couscous in an ovenproof dish
   and add the stock, leaving for 5 minutes
   until the stock is absorbed then add the
   dried fruit
4. Tip the chicken and all the juices into
   the couscous and toss together

> **Tip**: Try using quinoa with
> this recipe instead. At step 3,
> cook the quinoa according
> to packet instructions and add
> the sultanas/raisins afterwards.

# Chicken Skewers

Preparation Time: 10 minutes
Cooking Time: 30 minutes
**Serves 2 grown-ups and 2 little people**

## Ingredients
500g skinless and boneless chicken thigh fillets
  or 4 chicken breasts
1 long carrot
Leftover Pesto (page 117)

**TO SERVE:** rice, salad or vegetables of your choice

## Method
1. Preheat the oven to 200C/180C fan/gas 6
2. Cut the chicken into big chunks and coat with the Pesto
3. Cut the carrot into long, thin batons, these will be your skewers
4. Using a real skewer or paring knife, make a hole in the centre of each piece of chicken so the carrot can fit through the middle
5. Thread the chicken onto the carrot skewer, place on a greased baking tray and bake in the oven for 20–30 minutes or until the chicken is cooked

*Tip*: Experiment by adding other veggies to the skewer, such as halved baby tomatoes and courgette before popping in the oven.
*Leftovers*: Use any leftover chicken to make Chicken and Sweetcorn soup (page 158). Don't worry about it being coated in Pesto, it will add to the flavour.

# Baked Veggie Pasta

Preparation Time: 10 minutes
Cooking Time: 30 minutes
**Serves 2 grown-ups and 2 little people**

## Ingredients

½ butternut squash
1 courgette
1 red onion
1 red pepper
1 yellow pepper
2–3 sprigs of fresh thyme (1tsp dried)
Glug of olive oil
2 handfuls of dried or fresh pasta
Leftover Pesto (page 117)

## Method

1. Preheat the oven to 200C/180C fan/gas 6
2. Chop the vegetables and tip onto a baking tray
3. Drizzle with olive oil and thyme and using your hands toss it all together. Bake in the oven for 30 minutes
4. Meanwhile, cook the pasta according to the instructions on the packet
5. Once cooked, mix together the pasta and Pesto, stir in the vegetables and serve

# Chicken Kievs

Preparation Time: 15 minutes
Cooking Time: 40 minutes
**Serves 2 grown-ups and 2 little people**

## Ingredients

4 chicken breasts
6 cloves garlic, crushed (if you have l/o garlic butter
  use this for the filling instead of 3 of the garlic cloves)
4tbsp breadcrumbs
Glug of olive oil
2tbsp cream cheese
1tsp mixed herbs

## Method

1. Preheat the oven to 200C/180C fan/gas 6
2. Mix together half the garlic, breadcrumbs and oil and set aside
3. Mix together the cream cheese, mixed herbs and the rest of the garlic and set aside
4. Cut a slit in the chicken, stuff with the cream cheese mixture and close the edges to keep the mixture in; use a couple of toothpicks to seal shut if needed
5. Coat the chicken in the breadcrumb mixture, pop on a baking tray and bake in the oven for 30–40 minutes until the chicken is cooked through

*Tip*: If you have any leftover garlic butter (page 120) you can use this instead of the cream cheese, garlic and herb mixture.

# Turkey Meatball Casserole

Preparation Time: 15 minutes
Cooking Time: 20 minutes
**Serves 2 grown-ups and 2 little people**

## Ingredients

450g turkey mince
1 onion (chopped)
2 garlic cloves (crushed)
1tsp fresh chilli or ½tsp dried chilli
1tsp paprika
1tsp basil
½tsp oregano
2 baking potatoes (peeled and chopped into chunks)
500g jar passata or 1 tin of chopped tomatoes
1tsp olive oil
300ml Beef or Vegetable Stock (page 116)

**TO SERVE:** quinoa, couscous or crusty bread

## Method

1. Mix the turkey mince, basil, paprika, chilli and oregano together in a bowl and shape into 10–12 balls
2. Heat the oil in a deep pan (which has a lid) over a medium heat
3. Pan fry the meatballs for several minutes until browned all over
4. Add the onions, garlic, potatoes, tomatoes or passata and stock to the pan, cover and leave to simmer for 15–20 minutes until the potatoes are tender

*Leftovers*: Use leftover meatballs in any of our recipes that ask for mince. Try using in Meaty Bolognese (page 125) or Mama's Lasagne (page 121) or just serve in a sandwich the next day.

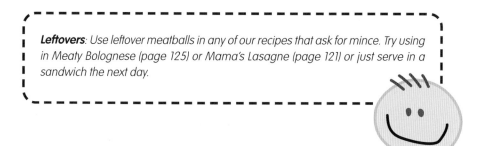

# Lamb Kebabs

Preparation Time: 10 minutes
Cooking Time: 15–20 minutes
**Serves 2 grown-ups and 1 little person**

## Ingredients

300g diced lamb
½ onion (chopped)
2 garlic cloves (crushed)
Ground black pepper
1tsp cumin
½tsp cayenne pepper
2 glugs of olive oil

**TO SERVE:** hummus, pitta bread and Yoghurt Dip (page 146)

## Method

1. Mix the onion, garlic, ground black pepper, cumin, cayenne pepper and one glug of olive oil together. Thoroughly rub into the lamb, cover and leave in the fridge to marinate for at least 20 minutes, overnight if possible
2. When ready to cook, preheat a griddle pan with another glug of olive oil and when hot add the lamb, turning until cooked through

*Leftovers*: Use any leftovers to make *Lamb Couscous Salad* (page 110).

# Lamb Couscous Salad

Preparation Time: 10 minutes
Cooking Time: 15–20 minutes
**Serves 2 grown-ups and 2 little people**

## Ingredients

Leftover Lamb Kebab
or....

**FOR THE LAMB:**
300g diced lamb or lamb chops
½tsp cayenne pepper
½tsp turmeric
1tsp cumin
½tsp cinnamon
Glug of olive oil
Ground black pepper

**FOR THE COUSCOUS SALAD:**
150g couscous, cooked according to packet instructions
½ red pepper (chopped)
½ red onion (chopped)
Glug of olive oil
Handful of spinach
Handful of chopped apricots
Handful of sultanas or currants

## Method

1. Mix the lamb spices and oil together and rub into the lamb, thoroughly coating the meat. Leave covered in the fridge for an hour or overnight if possible
2. Preheat a griddle pan, cook the lamb and set aside
3. To make the couscous salad, in a separate pan heat the oil and add the red onion and pepper, cooking for several minutes until the onions soften. Add the spinach and remove from the heat
4. Mix together the couscous and spinach mixture and toss in the rest of the couscous salad ingredients
5. Serve with the lamb chop on the side, or the lamb pieces tossed through the couscous salad

**Tip**: *This recipe works just as well with quinoa instead of couscous. Don't be afraid to experiment with your spices. Try adding some garlic, chilli or garam masala and change things up in the kitchen. Your family will love you for it.*

# Lamb or Beef Rissoles

Preparation Time: 30 minutes
Cooking Time: 20 minutes
**Serves 2 grown-ups and 1 little person**

## Ingredients

Leftover (cooked) Roast Dinner Lamb (page 165)
  or Slow Roast Beef Brisket (page 164)
Potatoes (the same quantity as meat,
  peeled and chopped)
1 onion (chopped)
1 clove of garlic (chopped)
1tsp mixed herbs
Black pepper to season
1 egg (beaten)
Plain flour (for dusting)
Glug of olive oil

## Method

1. Steam the potatoes for about 30 minutes until soft
2. Meanwhile, fry the garlic and onions in oil until the onions are soft
3. Place the onions, garlic and meat into a food blender and mince. Put in a big mixing bowl
4. Once cooked, mash the potatoes and add to the meat mixture. Squidge together using your hands
5. Add the beaten egg and mix in
6. Take a handful of the mixture and shape into a patty then coat with flour. Repeat until all the mixture has been used
7. To fry, add enough oil in a frying pan to cover the base and cook on a medium heat for about 20 minutes, turning once

> *Tip*: Try adding different herbs or spices to give the rissoles a different twist e.g. cumin and coriander or curry powder.

# Chicken and Tomato Bake

Preparation Time: 15 minutes
Cooking Time: 20 minutes
**Serves 1 grown-up and 1 little person**

## Ingredients

Leftover Chicken Cacciatore (page 128)
1 tin of chopped tomatoes
1tbsp olive oil or unsalted butter
1 yellow pepper (chopped)
1 red pepper (chopped)
1 onion (chopped)
Grated Cheddar cheese or mozzarella

**TO SERVE:** fresh seasonal vegetables

## Method

1. Preheat the oven to 200C/180C fan/gas 6
2. Tip the leftovers into an ovenproof dish. Add the chopped tomatoes to bulk up if necessary
3. Heat the oil or butter in a pan and fry the pepper and onion until softened, then add to the ovenproof dish, stirring well
4. Sprinkle with the grated cheese or mozzarella
5. Bake in the oven for 20 minutes

*Tip*: Even if the Chicken Cacciatore is mixed in with pasta, this still serves up well.

# Chicken Pancakes

Preparation Time: 30 minutes
Cooking Time: 30 minutes
**Serves 2 grown-ups and 2 little people**

## Ingredients

**TO MAKE THE BATTER:**
100g plain flour
1 egg (beaten)
Glug of olive oil
285ml full-fat milk

**TO MAKE THE FILLING:**
1tbsp butter
1 onion (chopped)
2–3tbsp full-fat milk
4 chicken breasts (sliced) or
  500g skinless, boneless chicken thigh fillets
4 handfuls of spinach
2 handfuls of grated cheese

**TO MAKE THE SAUCE:**
Glug of olive oil
1 onion (chopped)
2 cloves of garlic (chopped)
1 tin of chopped tomatoes
Squidge of tomato purée
Juice of ½ lemon

## Method

1. Preheat the oven to 180C/160C fan/gas 4
2. To make the filling, fry the onion in the butter until soft. Add the chicken and continue to cook until the chicken is brown and cooked through
3. Once cooked, mince the chicken, onion, spinach, cheese and milk in a blender or squidge with a potato masher
4. To make the sauce, fry the onion and garlic in the oil. Add the tinned tomatoes, tomato purée and lemon juice and season with some black pepper. Leave to simmer for 5 minutes
5. Meanwhile, make the pancakes by whisking the milk, egg and flour together. Add a ladle of mixture to hot oil in a frying pan and cook until golden, turning once
6. Once the pancakes are made, roll them with the filling in the middle and place in an ovenproof dish
7. Pour over the sauce. Cover with tin foil and bake in the oven for 15 minutes
8. Remove the foil and return to the oven for a further 15 minutes

---

*Adult add-on*: For a more flavoursome sauce add a splash of Worcester sauce at step 4.

*Development*: Chicken is a great source of protein and is rich in potassium and calcium, which are essential for the body's growth and maintenance.

*Development*: Spinach is rich in vitamins and minerals including vitamin K, which is key to bone health.

*Emma's Tip*: I always have a bag of spinach in the fridge and use it like a herb. Roughly chop the spinach and just before serving add to dishes like Bolognese (pages 76, 124 and 125) or Cottage Pie (page 86) and stir it through. It also makes a great topping for a Pizza (pages 122 and 123) or sprinkled in Sandwiches (page 52).

# Chicken/Beef Stock

Preparation Time: 10 minutes
Cooking Time: 2 hours
**The yield of stock will depend on the amount of bones you use and therefore the amount of water needed to cover them. Roughly speaking, using 1kg of beef bones will give 1–1.5l of stock**

## Ingredients

Leftover meat carcass
Cold water
Optional: carrot (chopped); leek (chopped); celery (chopped); onion (chopped); garlic
  (crushed); sprig of rosemary; sprig of thyme

## Method

1. Put the meat carcass, vegetables and herbs in a large saucepan with enough cold water to cover
2. Bring to the boil, skim the foam off the surface and discard
3. Simmer for 2 hours, occasionally skimming
4. Remove the bones from the pan and pour the liquid through a fine sieve so the stock falls into a large bowl
5. Allow the liquid to cool then chill. This will cause any fat to rise to the surface which you can then skim off once it has solidified
6. The remaining liquid stock, once cooled, will keep in the fridge for approximately 4 days. Alternatively, divide into smaller portions and freeze

*Tip*: *Home-made stock is a great base used for soups, stews and casseroles. It adds a lovely flavour that you know is full of goodness and salt-free.*
*Jane's Tip*: *I leave the stock to simmer for a lot longer until it becomes a nice, thick and richer concentrate. I freeze in old purée trays and add to cooking as needed.*

# Vegetable Stock

*Roughly chop 1 onion, 3 celery sticks, 2 leeks, 4 carrots, 2 bay leaves, 12 black peppercorns, a few sprigs of thyme and parsley and pop into a large pan. Add 1.7l water, simmer for 30 minutes, then strain through a fine sieve into a bowl.*

# Pesto

Preparation Time: 10 minutes
Cooking Time: 5 minutes
**Serves 2 grown-ups and 2 little people**

## Ingredients

2 handfuls of almonds
4 cloves of garlic (crushed)
2 handfuls of fresh basil
Glug of olive oil
Pinch of nutmeg
Optional: squeeze of lemon juice,
   Parmesan cheese

## Method

1.  Dry-fry the almonds in a hot frying pan until they start to brown
2.  In a food processor whizz all the ingredients until they form a paste, adding more oil until it reaches the consistency you desire

---

*Tip*: Pesto is a great pasta sauce and useful in so many recipes. If you have left-over purée trays, freeze into cubes and just pop out a couple as and when you need them.

*Tip*: You can easily burn nuts when frying them, so keep a close eye on the pan when cooking.

Chapter Seven

# Fakeaways

It's the weekend and before having children you might have treated yourself to a take-away; the trouble is that now you have little ones you need to think about feeding them too. So instead of opting to buy yourself a takeaway and cooking an additional meal for your children why not treat the whole family and indulge in a 'fakeaway'.

Depending on your mood, try different themed fakeaways. We've come up with some ideas for getting into the spirit and creating an authentic night in with your family. Why not try designing a menu and popping on some music in keeping with your fakeaway theme? Your children may like to pretend to ring and order the food and then help deliver it to the table. Put a selection of foods into separate bowls, place in the middle of the table and let everyone tuck in and help themselves. Older children may enjoy having a fakeaway when they have friends over to play and can take an active part in the preparation; they can decide on the courses, make a shopping list, go to the shops and even prepare the food with you.

# ITALIAN

**'A tavola non si invecchia'**
**('At the table with good friends**
**and family you do not become old')**

Your children may enjoy getting into the swing of the Italian night by colouring in some maps of Italy. They may be interested in seeing where Italy is on the map and seeing some pictures of some of its main landmarks, for example, the Leaning Tower of Pisa and the Coliseum. Or, your children may prefer the more energetic option of play fighting as gladiators to let off steam before sitting down to eat. Cover your table with a red and white checked tablecloth and, if safe, pop a candle in an empty wine bottle. Have some Pavarotti or Italian opera playing in the background and learn some Italian words to use as you tuck into your Italian feast:

*Ciao* means 'hello'
*Arrivederci* means 'goodbye'
*Grazie* means 'thank you'
*Sì* means 'yes'
*Per favore* means 'please'
As well as the recipes in this section, try also Bread Sticks (page 193).

# Garlic Bread (P/LB)

Preparation Time: 5 minutes
Cooking Time: 5 minutes
**Serves 2 grown-ups and 2 little people**

## Ingredients

1 baguette
2tbsp unsalted butter
1 clove of garlic (crushed)
1tbsp Parmesan (optional)

## Method

1. Preheat the oven to 200C/180C fan/gas 6
2. Make several 3cm thick diagonal slices in the bread, not quite cutting all the way through
3. Pop the butter in the microwave for a few seconds to soften so it is spreadable rather than melted
4. In a bowl mix together the butter, garlic and Parmesan (if using)
5. Pop a dollop of the butter mixture in between each slice of the bread and wrap the finished baguette in foil
6. Pop in the oven for several minutes until the butter has started to melt. Keep a close eye as it will overcook quickly

**Leftovers**: *if you have any leftover Garlic Butter mixture, make Chicken Kievs (page 107)*

# Mama's Lasagne

Preparation Time: 60 minutes
Cooking Time: 40 minutes
**Serves 2 grown-ups and 2 little people**

## Ingredients

**FOR THE MEAT SAUCE:**
2 tins of chopped tomatoes
2 big squidges of tomato purée
1 onion (chopped)
4 cloves of garlic (crushed)
500g lean beef mince
1tsp dried oregano
1tsp cayenne pepper
2tsp fresh basil (or 1tsp dried)

**FOR THE REST OF THE LASAGNE:**
12 dried lasagne sheets
2 handfuls of mozzarella cheese
1 handful of Parmesan cheese
2tbsp ricotta cheese and/or 2tbsp cottage cheese
1 egg

## Method

1. Cook the mince in a frying pan over medium heat until browned. Leaving the fat in the pan, remove the meat with a slotted spoon and set aside
2. Add the onions, garlic and cayenne pepper and cook in the fat over a medium heat until the onions soften
3. Stir in the oregano, cooked mince, tomato purée and chopped tomatoes and leave to simmer on a low heat for 45 minutes
4. Turn off the heat and add the basil
5. Preheat the oven to 200C/180C fan/gas 6
6. Mix the ricotta, cottage cheese and egg in a bowl and set aside
7. Into an ovenproof dish spoon some meat sauce then a layer of lasagne sheets, then spread some cheese mix over the top
8. Repeat step 7 a couple more times ending with the cheese layer
9. Sprinkle the mozzarella and Parmesan over the top and pop in the oven for 40 minutes until the cheese is melted and golden

## Pizza Base

If you prefer a regular pizza, here's a recipe for a pizza base.
Alternatively, pizza bases can be made in most bread makers.
Preparation Time: 15 minutes
**Makes 1 pizza base**

### Ingredients
200g plain flour
150ml warm water
2tbsp olive oil

### Method
1. Tip the oil and flour into a mixing bowl
2. Use your hands to mix together adding the water gradually to form a dough
3. If you add too much water, add more flour and stop when the dough is sticking together. If freezing, do so at this point
4. Roll out on a floured surface and continue with the recipe for Pitta Pizza (page 54)

**Variations for pizza toppings**: spread tinned tomatoes or tomato purée over the base and top with the following:
*Vegetarian Pizza*: onion, garlic, pepper, mushrooms (gently cooked in a bit of oil first to soften), sliced tomatoes and tinned sweetcorn
*Classic margarita*: mozzerella, cherry tomatoes
*Hawaiian*: diced cooked chicken breast, mushrooms, sweetcorn and pineapple chunks

***Adult add-on**: Scatter Parma ham and rocket over the top after it comes out of the oven.*
***Dave's Tip**: If you want a baby-friendly ham option for a more traditional Hawaiian pizza, submerge the uncooked ham in a pan of cold water, chucking in a couple of baking potatoes (peeled and halved) and bringing to the boil before baking in the oven as you normally would. The potatoes soak up the salt.*

# Puff Pastry Pizza (P/LB)

Preparation Time: 20 minutes
Cooking Time: 20 minutes
**Serves 1 grown-up and 1 little person**

## Ingredients

½ pack of puff pastry
½ pepper (chopped)
½ leek (sliced)
½ courgette (chopped)
½ onion (chopped)
4 mushrooms (sliced)
1 garlic clove (crushed)
Squidge of tomato purée or passata
Grated cheese
1tsp unsalted butter
Optional: cooked diced chicken, sweetcorn

## Method

1.  Preheat the oven to 200C/180C fan/gas 6
2.  Melt the butter in a pan and fry the onion, garlic, pepper, leek, courgette and mushrooms until soft
3.  Roll out the pastry to the desired size you want each pizza to be – you can roll out a family size pizza or smaller, individual ones
4.  Lay the pastry on a greased baking tray
5.  Spread some tomato purée or passata over the pastry base. Scatter the fried veggies on top, plus any additional toppings, and finish with a sprinkling of grated cheese
6.  Cook in the oven for 20 minutes

---

**Leftovers**: You can freeze the uncooked pizza after Step 5. With any leftover pastry, try making the Cheese Pastry Bites (page 60).
**Health**: Garlic is a natural antibiotic and may help with coughs and colds.
**Health**: Green peppers contain flavonoids, which strengthen capillaries, the smallest blood vessels, and may help speed up the healing of a bruise.

# Lentil Bolognese

Preparation Time: 20 minutes
Cooking Time: 50 minutes
**Serves 2 grown-ups and 2 little people**

## Ingredients

1tsp unsalted butter or olive oil
2 tins (800g) puy or green lentils
  (before embarking on this recipe,
  check the lentils don't need pre-cooking)
1 onion (chopped)
1 stick of celery (chopped)
1 red pepper (chopped)

2 cloves of garlic (crushed)
1 handful of mushrooms (chopped)
1 handful of spinach
Squidge of tomato purée
2 tins of chopped tomatoes
3–4 basil leaves (chopped)
  or ½tsp dried basil

**TO SERVE:** pasta; rice; baked potato

## Method

1. Heat the oil or butter in a large frying pan over a medium heat
2. Gently fry the onion, celery, red pepper and garlic
3. Once the onion has softened, add the mushrooms and spinach
4. After a couple of minutes add the tomato purée, chopped tomatoes, lentils and basil
5. Cover, turn the heat down and gently simmer for 40 minutes

*Tip*: Green and brown lentils are tricky to digest for little people so don't be surprised if you spot them in your baby's nappy.

*Adult add-on*: At step 4, just before simmering, add a couple of glugs of red wine and a splash of Worcester sauce to enhance the flavour and simmer for 5–10 minutes.

*Development*: Lentils are a great source of iron, which will help nourish the cells of your growing baby.

*Health*: Basil contains antibacterial properties and may help with coughs and colds.

*Health*: Split (red) lentils may be easier to digest as they are hulled and contain less fibre so will cause less wind and bloating.

*Health*: Lentils are good for preventing blood sugar levels from shooting up after a meal. They also help lower cholesterol so are good for the heart, benefiting the big people as well as the little ones. As lentils contain purines avoid serving to family members with a history of kidney stones or gout.

# Meaty Bolognese

Preparation Time: 20 minutes
Cooking Time: 50 minutes
**Serves 2 grown-ups and 2 little people**

## Ingredients

400g lean beef mince or turkey mince
1 onion (chopped)
1 red pepper (chopped)
2 cloves of garlic (crushed)
1 handful of mushrooms (chopped)
1 handful of spinach
2 squidges of tomato purée
2 tins of chopped tomatoes
1tsp unsalted butter or olive oil

**TO SERVE:** spaghetti; pasta; rice; baked potato; quinoa; couscous

## Method

1. Heat the oil or butter in a large pan and fry the onion, garlic and mince until the mince is browned
2. Stir in the red pepper, mushrooms and spinach
3. After a couple of minutes add the tomato purée and chopped tomatoes
4. Cover and turn the heat down so it gently simmers for 40 minutes
   See Lentil Bolognese (page 124) for more information on serving suggestions.

---

*Tip*: This recipe is very forgiving so don't worry if your quantities aren't exactly as stated. It's great for using up leftover veggies such as courgettes, aubergines, and green beans, just chop them up and add at stage 4 before simmering for 40 minutes.
*Leftovers*: Chilli Bolognese (page 76), Pizza Bolognese (page 77), Pasty Bolognese (page 78), Mama's Lasagne (page 121).
*Adult add-on*: After step 3 put your child's portion into a different saucepan and add a slosh of red wine (50–100ml) to the remaining Bolognese for a touch more flavour.

# Gnocchi

Preparation Time: 20 minutes
Cooking Time: 10 minutes
**Serves 2 grown-ups and 2 little people**

## Ingredients

Leftover mashed potato or
   2 baking potatoes (peeled)
3–4tbsp plain flour
1 egg
Glug of olive oil
1 garlic clove (crushed)
2tbsp unsalted butter
2tsp chopped fresh sage (1tsp dried)
Handful of freshly grated Parmesan
Black pepper

**TO SERVE:** Sweet Potato Wedges (page 201) and salad

## Method

1. If not using leftover mash, steam or boil the potatoes until tender but still firm (about 15 minutes). Be careful as overcooked potatoes will become heavy and tasteless. Drain
2. Add the garlic and black pepper then mash the potatoes with a fork or masher
3. In a large bowl mix the mashed potatoes, egg and olive oil. Knead in enough flour to make a soft dough
4. On a floured surface, roll the dough into a long rope. Cut the rope into 2cm pieces
5. Bring a large pot of water to the boil. Drop in the gnocchi, and cook until they float to the top, after about 3 to 5 minutes. Remove as soon as they float otherwise they'll fall apart
6. Melt the butter in a pan until it bubbles and turns golden (you're meant to overcook it)
7. Stir in the sage then toss the cooked gnocchi in the pan
8. Add some freshly grated Parmesan, stirring together until it melts

*Tip*: Sage is such an easy herb to grow in the garden and it's very hardy.
*Tip*: Instead of sage butter, try serving the Gnocchi with leftover tomato sauce (page 103).
*Tip*: If freezing, do so at the end of stage 5, once they're cut to size. Place on baking paper and pop in the freezer and, once frozen, store in a small Ziploc bag until needed.
*Leftovers*: Make a breakfast of Eggy Dumplings (page 103).
*Leftovers*: Whip-up some Gnocchi Patties. Shape the Gnocchi dough into patties, then heat some oil in a pan and cook through so they brown on both sides. Serve on rocket with some shaved Parmesan and some balsamic reduction.

# Chicken Cacciatore

Preparation Time: 30 minutes
Cooking Time: 40 minutes
**Serves 2 grown-ups and 2 little people**

## Ingredients

4 chicken breasts or 500g skinless
  and boneless chicken thigh fillets
1 onion (chopped)
Handful of mushrooms (sliced)
3 garlic cloves (crushed)
1tsp fresh chilli
1 tin of chopped tomatoes or 1 handful of fresh cherry tomatoes
4tbsp cream cheese or full-fat natural yoghurt
1tsp dried or a handful chopped fresh basil

**TO SERVE:** pasta, rice or mashed potatoes, and greens

## Method

1. Preheat the oven to 190C/170C fan/gas 5
2. Heat the oil in a deep pan and fry the onion, garlic and chilli until soft
3. Add the tomatoes and leave to simmer for 15 minutes
4. Stir in the cream cheese or yoghurt and basil, add the mushrooms and tip into a casserole or ovenproof dish
5. In the same frying pan, add some more oil and fry the chicken, cooking on both sides until golden. Ensure the heat is up high enough to brown rather than stew the chicken
6. Tip the chicken into the casserole dish, covering it with the sauce
7. Pop the lid on or cover with foil and bake in the oven for 30–40 minutes or until the chicken is cooked through

*Leftovers*: Use leftover roast chicken in this recipe. You can stir leftover sauce into a bowl of cooked pasta and serve with Garlic Bread (page 120) for a yummy, quick dinner. Or use any leftovers to make Chicken and Tomato Bake (page 113).

# Spaghetti Carbonara

Preparation Time: 20 minutes
Cooking Time: 40 minutes
**Serves 2 grown-ups and 2 little people**

## Ingredients

Handful of spaghetti
Glug of olive oil
Handful of broccoli florets
1 garlic clove (crushed)
2 eggs
1 onion (chopped)

Pinch of grated nutmeg
3tbsp milk or double cream
3tbsp Parmesan cheese
Ground black pepper to season
3tbsp fresh parsley (chopped)

## Method

1. Par-boil the broccoli in a large saucepan for a couple of minutes then remove and set aside but leave the water in the pan
2. Add the spaghetti to the water and cook according to the packet instructions
3. Once the broccoli has cooled, chop into small pieces
4. In a separate pan on a medium heat, warm the olive oil and add the onion, garlic and broccoli, stirring until the onion softens
5. In a separate bowl mix the eggs, milk or cream, cheese, nutmeg and black pepper together
6. Drain the pasta and pop into a pan on a medium heat; pour over the sauce and mix, stirring until the egg stiffens
7. Add the broccoli mixture, scatter with the chopped parsley and serve

*Leftovers*: We wouldn't recommend reheating carbonara as the eggs will set long before the cheese re-melts. So, if you have just the sauce (and not spaghetti) make a wonderful Frittata by heating a little butter in a frying pan and cooking the sauce. The eggs will stiffen causing it all to stick together like an omelette. Yummy! However, if you've mixed the spaghetti and sauce together try making a Pasta Gratin (page 101).

*Adult add-on*: Chop 3–4 bacon rashers into chunks and fry or grill. Once you've served your little one hers, mix the bacon into the pan at step 7 and serve.

# MEXICAN

### '*Comiendo entra la gand*'
### ('Appetite comes with eating')

Dig out your Latin music and set up a Mexican themed party – any music with some guitars and rhythm will surely get you in the swing. If you've got a cactus in the house this could make great table centrepiece and tipping some uncooked rice or beans into food storage containers makes good maracas for your little ones to shake. Wearing hats you can pretend are sombreros will get you in the spirit. We like to play bucking broncos beforehand where little one rides around on our backs and gets thrown onto the sofa, but it will all depend on the age of your children as to whether this is suitable. If you want to be a little more extravagant, make a piñata or your own Aztec masks whilst waiting for your Fakeaway to 'arrive'.

To add more to your Mexican night, why not try serving up some corn on the cobs, boiled or steamed. Little teethers can enjoy getting their teeth into one of these.

Now can be a fun time to learn some Spanish words:

*Hola* means 'hello'
*Adiós* means 'goodbye'
*Gracias* means 'thank you'
*Sí* means 'yes'
*Por favor* means 'please'

# Bean Burgers (P/LB)

Preparation Time: 10 minutes
Cooking Time: 15 minutes
**Makes 6–8 bean burgers**

## Ingredients

2 tins of kidney beans (drained and rinsed)
50g breadcrumbs
1 onion
½tsp fresh chilli (chopped)
½tsp garlic (crushed)
½tsp cumin
1tsp fresh coriander (½tsp dried)
1 egg
2tbsp full-fat natural yoghurt
Ground black pepper to season
Squeeze of lime juice

**TO SERVE:** toasted burger bun; strips of pitta and avocado slices; Sweet Potato Wedges (page 201)

## Method

1. Preheat the grill to high
2. In a large bowl, squidge the beans with a potato masher
3. Add the breadcrumbs, chilli, coriander, garlic, onion, cumin and egg and mix together with your hands. If the mixture is a little wet, add more breadcrumbs
4. Divide and shape the mixture into roughly 8 burgers
5. If freezing, do so now. Otherwise pop on a greased non-stick baking tray and grill for around 5–8 minutes on each side until golden and crisp
6. Mix the yoghurt, lime juice and black pepper together, and serve as a dip with the burgers

*Tip*: If cooking from frozen, bake at 200C/180C fan/gas 6 for 20–30 minutes until cooked through.

*Tip*: This works well with all sorts of beans; try using pinto beans or even a tin of mixed pulses instead.

*Tip*: Be sure to oil the baking tray or grill pan otherwise your burgers will stick and fall apart when you try and turn them over.

*Leftovers*: Use any leftover uncooked bean mixture to make Beany Balls (page 103).

**Adult add-on**: Add 1tbsp of sweet chilli dipping sauce to the burger mixture at step 2 for a spicier flavour.

# Chilli Con Carne

Preparation Time: 30 minutes
Cooking Time: 1 hour
**Serves 2 grown-ups and 2 little people**

## Ingredients

Glug of olive oil
1 onion (chopped)
1 red or yellow pepper (chopped)
2 garlic cloves (crushed)
1tsp mild chilli powder
1tsp paprika
2tsp cumin
½tsp cinnamon
500g lean minced beef
300ml Beef Stock (page 116)
1 tin of chopped tomatoes
½tsp dried marjoram or oregano
3 big squidges of tomato purée
1 tin of red kidney beans (pre-cooked, drained and rinsed)

**TO SERVE:** plain rice; Parsnip Crisps (page 138); baked potato; pitta bread; couscous; quinoa

## Method

1. Heat the oil in a deep pan (which has a lid) over a medium heat
2. Add the onions and cook for a few minutes until soft
3. Stir in the garlic, pepper, chilli powder, paprika, cumin and cinnamon and cook for another 5 minutes, stirring occasionally
4. Add the mince, cooking until there are no more pink bits. You may need to turn the heat up a little bit to ensure the beef browns rather than stews
5. Stir in the stock, chopped tomatoes, tomato purée, dried herbs and ground black pepper
6. Bring to the boil, cover and reduce the heat so it gently simmers for around 20 minutes. Stir it occasionally and keep tasting. Add more water if it looks a little dry and check the heat is low enough for it to gently bubble. After 20 minutes of simmering it should look thick and gloopy. Add some plain flour if it needs thickening up
7. Add the kidney beans and bring to the boil again for around 10 minutes
8. Have a taste and check to see if you might need to add a little more chilli powder
9. Replace the lid, turn off the heat and leave it on the hob for 10 minutes for the flavours to infuse and then it's ready to serve

---

**Tip**: For an extra yummy garnish top with Guacamole (page 140) and a handful of grated cheese.

**Adult add-on**: At step 7, melt a small piece (about the size of your thumbnail) of plain dark chocolate into the sauce, for an authentic Mexican meal.

**Adult add-on**: Before step 5, add a large glass of red wine to the mince, allowing it to reduce to burn off the alcohol. Then continue with step 5, simmering for 2 hours before continuing as the recipe suggests. This does take a while but produces a great flavour, perfect if you have guests for dinner.

# Bean Chilli

Preparation Time: 15 minutes
Cooking Time: 30–40 minutes
**Serves 2 grown-ups and 2 little people**

## Ingredients

Glug of olive oil
1 onion (chopped)
1tsp fresh chilli (chopped)
2 garlic cloves (crushed)
2tsp cumin
1tsp mild chilli powder
400g black-eyed beans (pre-cooked, drained and rinsed)
400g red kidney beans (pre-cooked, drained and rinsed)
2 tins of chopped tomatoes

**TO SERVE:** Pancakes (page 174); wraps with shredded lettuce, Salsa (page 139) and Guacamole (page 140) for make-believe tacos

## Method

1. Heat the oil in a large frying pan and cook the onion and fresh chilli until soft
2. Add the garlic, chilli powder and cumin and cook for a few more minutes
3. Add the beans and tomatoes and simmer for 30–40 minutes until the sauce has thickened.
4. Add some plain flour to thicken or water if a little dry

**Tip**: Any beans will do; try haricot, borlotti or butter. Just remember to check to see if they need soaking and pre-cooking before embarking on this recipe. **Adult add-on**: Serve in taco shells.

# Fajitas

Preparation Time: 10 minutes
Cooking Time: 30 minutes
**Serves 2 grown-ups and 2 little people**

## Ingredients

Glug of olive oil
500g skinless and boneless chicken thigh fillets
  or 4 chicken breasts (cut into chunks)
1tsp mild chilli powder
1 onion (sliced)
1 red pepper (sliced)
1 tin of chopped tomatoes

**TO SERVE:** wraps with Crunchy Green Salad (page 210), Guacamole (page 140), Salsa (page 139) and grated cheese

## Method

1. Heat the oil in a large pan over a high heat
2. Add the chicken (it should sizzle) and cook until browned all over
3. Add the chilli powder, stir until the chicken is coated and cook for a couple more minutes
4. Scoop out the chicken with a slotted spoon and set aside
5. In the same pan, fry the onion and red pepper and cook until soft
6. Add the tomatoes and chicken, cover (if you can) and simmer for 15 minutes. Add some plain flour to thicken if necessary and check the seasoning, adding more chilli powder if necessary

*Tip*: Instead of using chicken, try prawns or strips of steak, or even a combination of them all. Replacing the meat with a tin of kidney beans will make this a vegetarian meal, or adding beans to the meat will make the mixture go further.

# Parsnip Crisps (P/LB)

Preparation Time: 5 minutes
Cooking Time: 10 minutes
**Serves 1 grown-up and 1 little person**

## Ingredients
2 parsnips
Glug of olive oil

**TO SERVE:** Salsa (page 139) and Guacamole (page 140)

## Method
1. Preheat the oven to 200C/180C fan/gas 6
2. With a potato peeler, shave thin layers of parsnip lengthways and place in a bowl
3. Drizzle with the olive oil and toss until lightly coated
4. Lay out on a baking sheet and bake in the oven for around 5–10 minutes until golden and crispy

*Adult add-on*: Sprinkle with sea salt after cooking.

# Salsa (P/LB)

Preparation Time: 10 minutes
**Makes roughly 100ml of Salsa**

## Ingredients

4 large tomatoes (chopped finely)
Juice of 1 lime
½ red onion (chopped finely)
2 heaped tbsp fresh coriander (chopped)
1 green chilli (deseeded and chopped finely)
1 garlic clove (crushed)
Black pepper to season

## Method

1. Add all the chopped ingredients into a bowl and mix, or whizz them in a food processor
2. Pour over the lime juice, season with black pepper and stir well

---

**Leftovers**: This Salsa is a lovely bit on the side for many dishes such as Chicken & Apple Sausages (page 58) or Fish Fingers (page 55). It's a brilliant ketchup alternative.

## Guacamole (P/LB)

Preparation Time: 10 mins
**Makes roughly 50ml of Guacamole**

### Ingredients
1 ripe avocado (peeled and sliced)
2 cloves of garlic (crushed)
Squeeze of lemon juice
Black pepper to season

### Method
1. Blitz all the ingredients in a food processor. Alternatively mash them with a potato masher

> **Adult-add on**: Add some fresh chilli for a spicy kick. **Leftovers**: This makes a lovely sandwich filling.

# INDIAN

**'Rice tastes good when it is cooked properly, and talking is good when it is said at the right time'**
**Kashmiri proverb**

Throw a Bollywood party! Make the invitations and/or menus using your own take on *rangoli*, which is the art of Indian painting. Blend some sand with a variety of food colourings in a bowl or food mixer and, using a glue stick, make a pattern on the menu and sprinkle the sand onto it. The sand will stick, making a lovely pattern. Add flower petals and leaves for a warm touch. Store any left-over sand in a glass container with a cork to prevent hardening. Using washable felt tip pens or paint try drawing on each other's hands as if they are henna decorations.

# Onion Bhajis (P/LB)

Preparation Time: 5 minutes
Cooking Time: 5 minutes
**Serves 2 grown-ups and 1 little person**

## Ingredients

2 eggs
3 onions (sliced)
120g plain flour
1tsp ground coriander
1tsp cumin
Several glugs of cooking oil

## Method

1. Heat the oil in a deep frying pan or wok
2. Beat the eggs in a bowl and mix in the onions
3. Mix in the flour, ground coriander and cumin
4. To the hot oil, dollop in a large spoonful of the bhaji mixture and fry for 30–45 seconds, until golden-brown
5. Turn the bhaji over and fry for another 30–45 seconds, until crisp and golden-brown all over
6. Remove and drain on kitchen paper
7. Repeat with the remaining bhaji mixture ensuring the oil is hot before each batch

# Lamb Samosas

Preparation Time: 15 minutes
Cooking Time: 15 minutes
**Serves 2 grown-ups and 2 little people**

## Ingredients

500g minced lamb
1 onion (chopped)
2 garlic cloves (crushed)
½tsp chilli powder
1tsp ground turmeric
½tsp cumin
½tsp chilli
1tsp chopped fresh mint or coriander
½tsp fresh ginger (grated)
Squeeze of lemon juice
Filo pastry sheets
1 egg (whisked)
A glug of olive oil

## Method

1. Heat the oil in a frying pan and cook the garlic, onion, ginger and spices until the onion softens
2. Add the mince, stirring until it is cooked
3. Add the fresh herbs and lemon juice, remove from the heat and set aside
4. Cut the filo pastry sheet into 4 squares, each will be a samosa
5. Brush the filo pastry with the egg and spoon some filling into the centre
6. Fold the pastry diagonally across to the other corner and stick down, enveloping the mixture. Wrap the other corners round to make a triangle and coat the outside with egg
7. Either deep fry the samosas in a pan of hot cooking oil or pop in the oven on an oven-proof baking sheet and bake according to the instructions on the filo pastry packet

*Leftovers: Any leftover lamb mixture freezes really well and makes a lovely base for Meaty Bolognese (page 125) or you could try making Potato Curry (page 151).*

# Lamb Kofta

Preparation Time: 10 minutes
Cooking Time: 10 minutes
**Serves 2 grown-ups and 2 little people**

### Ingredients

500g minced lamb
1tsp cumin
2tsp ground coriander
2 garlic cloves (crushed)
1tbsp chopped mint
½tsp chilli (more if you want it spicier)
Juice of 1 lemon
1 egg (beaten)
1tsp olive oil

**TO SERVE:** pitta bread; Yoghurt Dip (page 146);
Mint Sauce (page 165); Crunchy Green Salad (page 210)

### Method

1. Mix together all the ingredients, apart from the oil, in a bowl with your hands
2. Divide and shape into 8 balls
3. Heat the oil in a griddle pan and cook for 4–5 minutes on each side until cooked through

*Tip*: Add breadcrumbs to the mixture to make it go a bit further.

# Mum's Chicken Curry

Preparation Time: 10 minutes
Cooking Time: 50 minutes
**Serves 2 grown-ups and 2 little people**

## Ingredients

Glug of olive oil
4 chicken breasts or 500g skinless and
  boneless chicken thigh fillets (diced)
1 onion (chopped finely)
1tsp cumin
2tsp ground coriander
1tsp turmeric
1tsp paprika
2 cloves of garlic (crushed)
½tsp fresh ginger (grated)
1 green chilli (deseeded and finely chopped)
Squeeze of lemon juice
75ml water or Chicken Stock (page 116)
400ml coconut milk
Fresh coriander to garnish

**TO SERVE:** rice; naan bread; chapattis

## Method

1. Heat the oil in a pan and fry the onions gently until soft
2. Add the cumin, ground coriander, turmeric and paprika and stir, then add the ginger, garlic and chilli
3. Add the chicken and cook until browned then add the lemon juice and cover with the water or stock and simmer for 20 minutes
4. Pour in the coconut milk, stir and bring to a simmer for a further 20 minutes
5. Sprinkle with freshly chopped coriander and serve

*Leftovers*: Make Curry Baked Rice by stirring together the leftover rice and curry. If you have any cooked roast chicken toss that and a few sliced mushrooms in too. Pop in an ovenproof dish, cover with mozzarella cheese and bake on 200C/180 fan/gas 7 until the cheese has turned golden brown.

*Tip*: The freezing of curry acts as a long term marinade so once it defrosts, the spices will be much more intense.

*Tip*: If your plastic storage boxes become stained from storing curry, use sterilizing fluid you may have used for bottles and teats. Leave immersed overnight and be sure to rinse thoroughly before using again.

## Yoghurt Dip

Preparation Time: 5 minutes
**Serves 2 grown-ups and 2 little people**

### Ingredients

3tbsp full-fat natural yoghurt
2tbsp chopped fresh mint
Big chunk of cucumber, peeled and grated
Ground black pepper

### Method

1. Press the grated cucumber into a sieve to remove as much water as possible
2. Chuck all the ingredients in a food processor and blitz

*Tip*: If the dip is still watery, run through a sieve again as this will produce a thicker dip.

# Chicken Biryani

Preparation Time: 20 minutes
Cooking Time: 1 hour
**Serves 2 grown-ups and 2 little people**

## Ingredients

Glug of olive oil
500g skinless and boneless chicken thigh fillets
  or 4 chicken breasts (cut into chunks)
2 cloves of garlic (crushed)
½tsp fresh chilli (1tsp dried)
1 onion (chopped)
1tsp mild curry powder
1tsp garam masala
250g uncooked rice
600ml Chicken or Vegetable Stock (page 116)
1 handful frozen peas

## Method

1. Heat the oil in a large pan (with a lid) and fry the chicken for 10 minutes until it begins to brown
2. Add the onion, garlic and chilli and cook for 5 more minutes until the onions soften
3. Add the rice, stock, curry powder and garam masala and bring to the boil
4. Cover the pan with a lid or foil and leave to simmer for 20–30 minutes until all the water has been absorbed
5. Turn off the heat, stir in the peas and replace the lid allowing the peas to cook through for another 5–10 minutes

---

*Tip*: Don't worry if you overcook the rice as it will go quite stodgy, which makes it easier for your baby to pick up with his hands and allows it to stick to the spoon.
**Leftovers**: Use the leftover rice to make Arancini di Riso (page 84).
**Adult add-on**: For a hotter curry, use hot curry powder and adjust quantity to taste.

# Chicken Curry (Spice-Rack Slammer)

Preparation Time: 20 minutes
Cooking Time: 40 minutes
**Serves 2 grown-ups and 2 little people**

## Ingredients

Glug of olive oil
500g skinless and boneless chicken thigh fillets
    or 4 chicken breasts (cut into pieces)
250ml full-fat natural yoghurt
2 onions (chopped)
3 cloves of garlic (crushed)
1tsp grated fresh ginger or 2tsp ground ginger
1tsp cumin
1tsp turmeric
1tsp ground coriander
½tsp cayenne pepper
½tsp ground fennel seeds
1tsp garam masala
500ml water
1 tin of chopped tomatoes

**TO SERVE:** rice; naan bread; chapattis

## Method

1. Heat the oil in a pan until hot and fry the chicken pieces for 5 minutes until starting to brown, then remove from the pan and set aside
2. Lower the heat and add the onion, garlic and ginger and cook for 8–10 minutes until the onions are soft
3. Add the cumin, turmeric, ground coriander, cayenne pepper, fennel seeds and 1tbsp water and stir for 2 minutes
4. Add the tomatoes and yoghurt and stir, then add the chicken and the remaining water, turn up the heat and bring to the boil
5. Sprinkle with garam masala, reduce the heat and simmer with the lid on for 20 minutes until the chicken is cooked through

*Tip*: This recipe needs a lot of attention and time at the cooker, so is best saved for making during naptime.

*Tip*: A lid tends to help prevent the liquid from evaporating too much. If your pan hasn't got a lid, you may need to add a little more water to the recipe at step 4. Experiment and see how it goes.

*Tip*: If storing cooked rice for the next day, don't leave it at room temperature for too long as this can cause bacteria to build and increases the risk of food poisoning. Cool the rice and have it in the fridge within an hour. We suggest running it under the tap and popping in a food storage container. Keep it in the fridge for no more than a day until reheating. As with reheating any food, always check that it's steaming hot all the way through, and avoid reheating more than once.

*Leftovers*: If reheating the curry on the hob, be aware that the water will evaporate, making for a thicker curry. If you haven't much sauce to begin with reheating in the microwave may be better.

*Leftovers*: We love to spoon leftover chicken curry into a tortilla wrap. Add a dollop of natural yoghurt and some shredded lettuce and watch your little one get very messy!

*Adult add-on*: For a milder curry, serve on the day of cooking. For grown-ups with a spicier palate, pop in the fridge overnight and serve the following day. The spices will mature overnight so it will be a hotter curry the next day.

# Sammy's Saag Aloo (Vegetable Curry)

Preparation Time: 15 minutes
Cooking Time: 15 minutes
**Serves 2 grown-ups and 2 little people**

## Ingredients

Glug of vegetable oil
2 baking potatoes (peeled and cut into chunks)
2 onions (chopped)
2 cloves of garlic (crushed)
½ cauliflower (broken into florets)
1 handful of spinach
2tsp cumin
2tsp coriander
2tsp chilli powder
1tsp turmeric
1tsp ginger
1tsp cinnamon
1tsp cardamom
150ml water

## Method

1. Steam or par-boil the potatoes for 5–10 minutes to soften
2. Meanwhile, fry the spices in the oil in a large frying pan for 2–3 minutes until just starting to brown
3. Add the onions and garlic and fry until starting to soften and brown
4. Add the water, potatoes and cauliflower to the pan and allow to simmer for 10 minutes
5. Add the spinach and turn the heat off but leave the pan on the stove. Once the spinach wilts remove from the heat and serve

*Tip*: If you don't have all of these spices try using 1tsp garam masala, 1tsp turmeric, 1tsp ground ginger instead.
*Tip*: The effect of freezing on vegetables is that it makes them softer over time. When defrosting, consider adding some extra steamed cauliflower and potatoes to vary the texture.
***Katie's tip***: When buying fresh ginger, I buy a large chunk and give it a quick rinse, chop it into around 1cm chunks and freeze. Frozen ginger shreds/grates really easily.

## Potato Curry

Preparation Time: 5 minutes
Cooking Time: 15–20 minutes
**Serves 1 grown-up and 1 little person**

### Ingredients
Leftover Samosa filling (page 142) (optional)
1tsp garam masala
1 or 2 baking potatoes (peeled and chopped)
250ml Vegetable or Beef Stock (page 116)

### Method
1. Place all the ingredients in a large pan and leave to simmer for 15–20 minutes until the potatoes are cooked through

# CHINESE

**'Anything that walks, swims, crawls, or flies with its back to heaven is edible'**
**Cantonese saying**

Get out the chopsticks and have some fun with your Chinese fakeaway. Decorate some pieces of paper and fold them up to make fans and decorate your menu with dragons and Chinese symbols. If you have an orchid make it the centrepiece of the table. If your children are old enough play pin the tail on the dragon. If it's a special occasion you may even choose to light a Chinese lantern.

# Sweet and Sour Chicken/Prawn

Preparation Time: 20 minutes
Cooking Time: 50 minutes
**Serves 2 grown-ups and 2 little people**

## Ingredients

Glug of olive oil
100ml soda water (from the fridge)
100ml cold water
140g self-raising flour
1tbsp cornflour
500g skinless and boneless chicken thigh fillets/chicken breasts/prawns
1 red pepper (deseeded and chopped into chunks)
1tsp fresh chilli (chopped finely)
400g tinned pineapple chunks (drained and juice reserved)
Squeeze of lemon juice
100ml grape juice
100ml white wine vinegar or malt vinegar

**TO SERVE:** rice

## Method

1. Put the red pepper, chilli and pineapple juice in a saucepan and bring to the boil, simmering for 10 minutes. Purée in a food processor
2. Return the purée to the pan adding the pineapple chunks, lemon juice, grape juice and vinegar
3. Simmer for 30–40 minutes until reduced and sticky
4. Meanwhile, fill a large pan with oil to around ½cm depth and place on a high heat
5. Make the batter by whisking the soda water, 100ml cold water and the flour together and set aside
6. Coat the chicken or prawns with the cornflour then dip into the batter
7. Carefully lower the chicken or prawns into the oil, adjusting the heat to keep it frying for around 5–10 minutes, turning once to ensure it's cooked through
8. When cooked, remove and drain on some paper towel
9. To serve either mix the chicken/prawns and sauce together or try serving separately as chicken/prawn dippers

# Special Fried Rice (P/LB)

Preparation Time: 10 minutes
Cooking Time: 10 minutes
**Serves 1 grown-up and 1 little person**

## Ingredients

Leftover Scrambled Egg (page 40)
Leftover or freshly cooked rice
1 onion (chopped)
1 pepper (chopped)
1tsp unsalted butter
1 handful of frozen peas
Optional: cooked chicken, cooked turkey, cooked peas,
    cooked sweetcorn

## Method

1. Melt the butter in a large pan and fry the onion until soft
2. Stir in the pepper, scrambled egg, rice and peas and cook for 5 minutes until the peas have softened
3. Add any optional ingredients and heat through

*Leftovers*: Use any leftover cooked rice to make a quick dessert of Banana Rice Pudding (page 186).

## Fish Cakes

Preparation Time: 45 minutes
Cooking Time: 20 minutes
**Serves 2 grown-ups and 1 little person**

### Ingredients

Leftover cooked Fish Fingers (page 55)
1 small tin of salmon or tuna
4 potatoes
1tsp unsalted butter
2–3tbsp plain flour
Optional: chopped spinach, grated cheese,
   grated courgette, chopped broccoli

## Method

1. Peel and quarter the potatoes then boil or steam for 30 minutes until soft enough for mashing
2. Drain and mash the potatoes with some butter
3. Preheat the oven to 200C/180C fan/gas 6
4. Mix the leftover Fish Fingers, salmon or tuna and any extra ingredients into the mash
5. Add the flour, 1tbsp at a time, until the mixture feels less sticky and becomes light and fluffy
6. Place the mixture on a floured surface and shape into small circles or wedges
7. Pop on a baking tray and bake in the oven for 20 minutes, turning once, until golden on both sides

*Tip*: These can be pan-fried if you prefer by melting a knob of butter in a frying pan over a medium heat and frying on both sides until golden brown.

*Health*: Potatoes may help improve your baby's sleep as they clear away amino acids that might interfere with your baby's slumber.

*Health*: Salmon and tuna contain niacin, which helps balance your baby's digestive system.

*Adult add-on*: Stir in 1tbsp sweet chilli dipping sauce before frying for a spicy touch.

# Lemon Chicken Stir Fry

Preparation Time: 15 minutes
Cooking Time: 20 minutes
**Serves 2 grown-ups and 2 little people**

## Ingredients

500g chicken breast or skinless
   and boneless chicken thigh fillets
Glug of olive oil
1 shallot (chopped)
2 cloves of garlic (crushed)
2tsp ginger (chopped)
1 small green chilli (deseeded and chopped finely)
1 stalk of lemongrass (finely chopped)
Handful of mange tout (roughly chopped)
8 baby corns (roughly chopped)
4 large mushrooms (finely sliced)
1 red pepper (sliced)
150ml Chicken Stock (page 116)
1tbsp cornflour
1tbsp water
1tbsp honey
Juice of ½ lemon

**TO SERVE:** noodles; rice

## Method

1. Heat some oil over a low heat in a wok or large frying pan
2. Add the shallot, ginger, garlic, chilli and lemongrass and cook slowly for a few minutes until the shallot softens
3. Add the chicken then turn up the heat and cook for about 10 minutes, ensuring the chicken is cooked through
4. Meanwhile, mix the water and cornflour together then add it to the stock and stir
5. Once the chicken is cooked pour in the stock, add the honey and lemon juice and stir for a few minutes and allow the stock to reduce (you may want to add a splash of water if the sauce becomes too thick)
6. Add the vegetables and cook for a further 3–5 minutes

*Leftovers*: Use any leftovers to make a delicious wrap. Take a wrap and place some shredded Romaine lettuce, Guacamole (page 140) and the leftover Lemon Chicken Stir Fry in it and enjoy!

# Chicken and Sweetcorn Soup

Preparation Time: 5 minutes
Cooking Time: 15 minutes
**Serves 2 grown-ups and 1 little person**

## Ingredients
Handful of leftover cooked chicken (or turkey)
Handful of tinned or frozen sweetcorn
Splash of cream or milk
600ml Vegetable or Chicken Stock (page 116)

## Method
1. Tip all the ingredients into a saucepan and cook over a medium heat until the meat is cooked through

*Tip*: Adding a little cornflour dissolved in water will thicken the soup.
*Tip*: Chunky Bread (page 39) served alongside the soup will act as a great spoon.

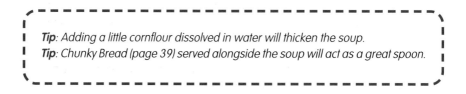

# BRITISH

**'Food, glorious food! Hot sausage and mustard!
While we're in the mood – cold jelly and custard!'
Charles Dickens, *Oliver Twist***

Get out the bunting, dress up as pearly kings and queens and, if your children are old enough, maybe you could enjoy a game of Monopoly and enjoy visiting the famous streets of London. Decorated doilies make lovely place settings and serving water to your guests out of a lovely teapot can give an authentic feel to your British fakeaway. Dust off the vinyl and play some Beatles, Rolling Stones, David Bowie, Adele or Coldplay and enjoy a night of appreciating some British artists.

Last time we each chose a country in Great Britain and had to research it. Our Scottish child wore a tartan skirt and pranced around playing the recorder and doing some Scottish dancing. We also had a great game of tug of war at our Highland games with a shot put contest using a soft ball we had to throw into a hula-hoop.

We coloured in some pictures of dragons with our Welsh guest who also brought along a rugby ball to exert some energy in the garden before we sat down for our lovely dinner. Our Irish dinner guest had researched St Patrick and gave a lovely demonstration of Irish dancing which we all had a go at – lots of fun before sitting down to enjoy our family feast!

# Scotch Eggs (P/LB)

Preparation Time: 20 minutes
Cooking Time: 10 minutes
**Serves 2 grown-ups and 1 little person**

## Ingredients

4 sausages (skinned) or sausage meat
1tsp sage
½tsp thyme
Ground black pepper
Pinch of cayenne pepper
4 slices of bread
5 eggs
2tbsp plain flour
Glug of olive oil

## Method

1. Toast the bread and then whizz in a food blender to make breadcrumbs and set aside in a shallow bowl

2. Hard boil 4 of the eggs for 5 minutes. Peel once cooled and set aside

3. Whisk the remaining egg in a shallow bowl and set aside

4. Put the sausage meat into a bowl and add the cayenne pepper, sage, thyme and black pepper and mix thoroughly; divide the mixture and shape into four thin patties

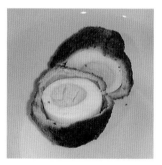

5. Spread the flour on a large plate and dust a patty in the flour, place an egg in the middle and wrap the sausage meat around the egg so it fully envelops it, leaving no gaps

6. Roll the meaty egg in the flour to coat, dip in the whisked egg and then coat with the breadcrumbs; repeat with the remaining three eggs

7. Heat some oil in a frying pan and shallow fry the eggs for several minutes, turning constantly until golden brown all over

# Sausage Rolls (P/LB)

Preparation Time: 30 minutes
Cooking Time: 30 minutes
**Serves 2 adults and 1 little person**

## Ingredients

Leftover Chicken and Apple Sausages (page 58)
½ packet of puff pastry
1 egg (beaten)
1tbsp plain flour

## Method

1. Roll the pastry on a floured surface into a rectangle. When rolling, be quite rough with it as this encourages the layers to separate and the pastry to puff up when cooked
2. Cut the rectangle into strips, the width of your sausages and brush with the beaten egg
3. Place a sausage at one end of the rectangle and roll it up. Only roll it once so there is a single layer of pastry around the sausage, otherwise you might find the pastry doesn't cook and goes soggy
4. Pop in the fridge for 20 minutes for the pastry to harden. If freezing, do so now
5. Pre-heat the oven to 200C/180C fan/gas 6
6. Remove from the fridge and prick the tops with a fork and brush with more egg
7. Pop in the oven for 25–30 minutes until they begin to turn golden and crispy

*Tip*: An alternative to sausage meat: put some frying steak in Beef Stock (page 116) and leave it overnight in a slow cooker for 6–8 hours on low. Use spoonfuls of the tender meat as your Sausage Roll filling.
**Leftovers**: Use any leftover pastry to make a Cheese and Tomato Tartlet (page 61).

# Mini Meaty Pasties (P/LB)

Preparation Time: 30 minutes
Cooking Time: 55 minutes
**Serves 2 grown-ups and 2 little people**

## Ingredients

225g Shortcrust Pastry (page 71)
200g stewing beef or casserole beef
1 onion (chopped)
2 small potatoes (peeled and sliced)
½ swede (diced)
1 egg (beaten)
1tbsp plain flour
1tsp unsalted butter

## Method

1. Preheat the oven to 220C/200C fan/gas 7
2. Melt the butter in a frying pan. Fry the onions until soft and add the beef, cooking until browned
3. Add the potatoes and swede and continue to cook until the vegetables are soft
4. Roll out the pastry on a lightly floured surface and cut into 4 circles. A mug or dinner plate can be used as a handy template if you haven't got a pastry cutter
5. Brush a pastry circle with the egg and put a spoonful of pasty mixture in the centre, fold over one side of the circle to the other, making a half circle, and pinch the edges together to seal. Brush the outside with more egg
6. Repeat step 5 to make the remaining three pasties
7. If freezing, do so now otherwise place on a greased baking tray and bake for 10 minutes then reduce the oven temperature to 180C/160C fan/gas 4 and cook for 45 minutes

*Tip*: Set your oven timer to remind you to turn the oven down after 10 minutes.
*Health*: Swede is high in fibre, stimulating regular bowel movements, and may help relieve constipation.
*Health*: Potatoes contain vitamin E, which may help relieve the symptoms of a blocked nose or hay fever.

# Welsh Rarebit

Preparation: 5 minutes
Cooking Time: 5 minutes
**Serves 1 grown-up and 1 little person**

## Ingredients

2 handfuls of grated Cheddar cheese
1 egg yolk
Slosh of cream or milk
2 slices of toast

## Method

1. Preheat the grill
2. Mash the cheese, egg, cream or milk together in a bowl
3. Spread the mixture over the toast ensuring you reach the edges
4. Pop under the grill for a couple of minutes until the cheese is golden and bubbling

> ***Adult add-on***: *At stage 2, add a couple of drops of Worcestershire sauce and Tabasco sauce to spice things up a bit.*

# Slow Roast Beef Brisket

Preparation Time: 20 minutes
Cooking Time: 3½ hours
**Serves 2 grown-ups and 2 little people**

## Ingredients

1kg beef brisket
1 onion (chopped)
1 handful of carrots (chopped into batons)
Glug of vegetable oil
100ml Beef Stock (page 116)

**TO SERVE:** roast potatoes, steamed seasonal vegetables

## Method

1. Preheat your oven to 160C/140C fan/gas 3
2. Heat the oil in a large pan over a medium heat
3. Add the beef and fry, turning until brown on all sides
4. Put the beef in a casserole dish and scatter the carrots around the edge then set aside
5. Tip the fat out of the pan and add the stock and onion, bringing to the boil
6. Pour the stock and onions over the beef and cover with a lid
7. Cook in the oven for approximately 3 hours until tender
8. Remove from the oven and leave to rest for 30 minutes before serving

*Tip*: Cooking the meat slowly allows the tougher, less expensive cuts of beef, such as brisket, to tenderize so they are less chewy for your baby to eat.
**Leftovers**: Use any leftover beef for Sandwiches (page 52) or Rissoles (page 112).
**Tara's Tip**: We often pop the brisket in the oven and the veggies in the steamer and go out for a walk. Having dinner waiting when we return leaves me feeling a little smug.

# Lamb Roast Dinner

Preparation Time: 20 minutes
Cooking Time: 3½ hours
**Serves 2 grown-ups and 2 little people**

## Ingredients

1.5kg shoulder of lamb
Glug of olive oil
1 bunch of fresh rosemary (chopped)
1 whole bulb of garlic, cloves crushed
Ground black pepper to season

**FOR MINT SAUCE:**
25g fresh mint leaves (chopped)
3tsp grape or apple juice
1tbsp boiling water
2tbsp vinegar

**TO SERVE:** steamed seasonal vegetables and potatoes

## Method

1. Preheat your oven to a high temperature
2. Score the fatty side of your lamb with a sharp knife and rub in the oil and season with black pepper
3. Place in a roasting tin and cover the lamb with the rosemary and garlic; cover loosely with tin foil
4. Turn the oven down to 170C/150C fan/gas 3 and cook the lamb for about 3.5 hours (when the meat falls apart easily you know it is cooked)
5. Make the mint sauce by mixing all the ingredients together (allow the sauce to stand for about 20 minutes to allow the mint to infuse)

*Leftovers:*
*Use any leftover lamb to make Sandwiches (page 52) or Rissoles (page 112)*

# Fish and Chips

Preparation Time: 15 minutes
Cooking Time: 45 minutes
**Serves 2 grown-ups and 2 little people**

## Ingredients

4 baking potatoes
Glug of olive oil
4 pieces of fish (such as skinless
  and boneless haddock, hake or cod fillet)
2tbsp plain flour
1 egg white
2tbsp soda water
1 ice cube
Several big glugs of cooking oil

**TO SERVE:** wedges of lemon, peas

## Method

1. Peel the potatoes and cut into big chunky chips. Steam or boil for no more than 5 minutes
2. Drain the chips and rough them up in a saucepan then leave to dry on a clean tea towel
3. Preheat the oven to 220C/200C fan/gas 7
4. Pour some olive oil into a roasting tin and heat in the oven for 10 minutes. Once hot, spread the chips out carefully in the roasting tin
5. Bake for 15–20 minutes, remove and turn the chips in the oil, then bake for another 15–20 minutes until golden and crispy. Drain on paper towels
6. Meanwhile, tip 1tbsp of flour onto a plate and coat each piece of fish
7. Pour enough cooking oil to cover the bottom of a heavy, medium non-stick wok or wok-shaped pan to about a depth of ½cm, and heat on high until very hot
8. Put the rest of the flour in a mixing bowl and whisk in the fizzy water; add the ice cube
9. Whisk the egg white until frothy and bubbly then lightly whisk it into the flour mixture (try to keep it as light and bubbly as possible)
10. Dip the fish in the batter to coat, then lower into the hot oil
11. Fry for 5–6 minutes, carefully turning the fish so it is golden all over
12. Drain on kitchen paper and repeat for the other fish pieces

*Tip*: The key to this recipe is to keep the batter cold and oil hot. Avoid adding too many pieces of fish at once.

*Tip*: If a fish fillet is too big a portion size, cut into chunks and fry as goujons – great for picnics.

*Tip*: Use this batter to make tempura with prawns, calamari, sliced courgette, broccoli or cauliflower.

*Tip*: Don't bin the egg yolk; why not use it to make a pudding of Baked Custard (page 187)?

*Tip*: Line a piece of newspaper with some greaseproof paper and roll to make a cone shape. Serve some fish and chips in the cone.

# Toad In The Hole With Onion Gravy

Preparation Time: 40 minutes
Cooking Time: 30 minutes
**Serves 2 grown-ups and 2 little people**

## Ingredients

6 leftover Chicken and Apple Sausages (page 58)
100g plain flour
2 eggs
½tsp English mustard powder (optional)
300ml full-fat milk
2 onions (chopped)
500ml Beef Stock (page 116)
1tsp dried thyme or sage
Glug of olive oil

**TO SERVE:** mashed swede

## Method

1. Preheat the oven to 200C/180C fan/gas 6
2. Mix the flour, mustard powder (if using), egg, milk and herbs together to make a smooth batter, set aside in the fridge until needed
3. Choose a roasting tin that suits the number of sausages you have – a loaf tin we find is perfect for 6. There should only be a small gap between the sausages when all laid out
4. Put the sausages in the tin and drizzle with the oil, coating the sausages and base of the tin; pop in the oven for 20 minutes to get the pan sizzling hot
5. Ensure the kids are out of the way at this point. Remove the tray and pour over the chilled batter – it will bubble and spit a bit as it meets the hot fat so be careful
6. Pop back in the oven for 30 minutes on a low shelf until the batter is cooked through, risen and crisp. Poke with a knife; it should be set, not runny
7. To make the gravy, heat some oil in a frying pan and add the onions. Cook for around 15 minutes until softened
8. Add a splash of apple juice and cook for a further 5 minutes
9. Add 1tbsp plain flour, coating the onions and cook for 2 minutes, stirring continuously until no flour is left
10. Pour in the stock, stirring to make a smooth sauce and allow to bubble for 5 minutes to thicken
11. Once cooked, cut the toad in the hole into large wedges and serve with the gravy spooned over

> **Adult add-on**: Try using spicier Cumberland sausages, and add 1tsp brown sugar to the onion gravy at step 8.

Chapter Eight

# Pudding

One of the most liberating yet frustrating things about being a parent is that there is no set way to do things and the same applies to feeding. Whether or not you choose to offer your little one a pudding is up to you. Some decide to offer pudding at the same time as the main meal so as not to distinguish between the two. Others only offer puddings on a Sunday and some not at all. The choice is yours.

Puddings are an optional extra when it comes to mealtimes, yet simple yoghurt for dessert can give the reassurance that your child is getting protein and calcium, especially when she starts to reduce her milk feeds.

Humans have a natural preference toward sweet flavours. They conjure up a feeling of comfort and security and are subconsciously associated with mother's milk. Sweetness sends a positive message to your brain that everything is all right but to get that feeling you don't need to add teaspoons of refined sugar to a dessert. Sweetness can come from natural sources such as ripe fruit and sweet tubers and we hope by using these recipes you will enjoy serving and eating delicious desserts, knowing you are not feeding your child pointless, factory-processed, refined sugar.

# Natural Fruity Yoghurt

Preparation Time: 5 minutes
**Serves 1 little person**

## Ingredients
3tbsp full-fat natural yoghurt
1tsp Fruit Purée (page 36) or Fruit Compote (page 35)

## Method
1. Mix some yoghurt with the purée or compote and serve
2. A tasty and cheap alternative to pre-packaged yoghurt pots, which are frequently sugar filled.

> *Tip*: Yoghurt is a messy business and not for the faint-hearted.
> *Tip*: St Dalfour fruit spread is a nice alternative to jam and contains no added sugar. It is available in the preserves section in most major supermarkets and is scrummy stirred in to some yoghurt.
> *Leftovers*: Put in the freezer and then chop into chunks. Makes a yummy breakfast, snack or pudding.
> *Health*: The proteins in milk, responsible for many dairy allergies, are largely broken down as it matures so dairy-sensitive babies may be able to tolerate yoghurt.

# Cheesecake

Preparation Time: 5 minutes
**Serves 1 little person**

## Ingredients

Leftover Oaty Bar (page 48) or Breakfast Bar (page 43)
1tbsp full-fat natural yoghurt
1tbsp Fruit Compote (page 35), Fruit Purée
   (page 36) or St Dalfour fruit spread

## Method

1. Place a deep cookie cutter or chef's ring
   on a plate and load in some of the
   crumbled Oaty Bar or Breakfast Bar,
   patting down to make the base
2. Sieve the yoghurt and spoon the
   creamier, thicker part on top of the base
3. Top with the Fruit Compote, Fruit Purée
   or St Dalfour fruit spread
4. Carefully remove the cookie cutter. You
   might find you have to use a spoon to
   gently push down on the cake to remove it and then serve

*Tip*: Lightly oil or grease the cutter/ring beforehand, to make it easier to remove.
**Adult add-on**: These make a wonderfully easy dinner party dessert. Soak some
digestive biscuits in apple juice to make them clump together and use in place of
the Oaty Bar or Breakfast Bar. Use cream cheese in place of the yoghurt and a
larger cookie cutter for a bigger portion. For an extra touch (and to hide the faults)
top with some chopped berries to match the choice of fruit topping.

# Strawberry Lollies

Preparation Time: 5 minutes
Freezing Time: 4–6 hours
**Serves 1 little person**

## Ingredients

Glug of full-fat milk
1 handful fresh or frozen strawberries

## Method

1. Put the ingredients in a blender and whizz together
2. Freeze in lolly moulds

> *Tip*: If you don't have lolly moulds, pour the mixture into ice cube trays and pop in a small plastic spoon to act as the handle. The spoons that come with baby medicines are an ideal size.
> *Tip*: Ideal for using up old fruit or milk that's approaching its use-by date.
> *Development*: Strawberries are a great source of immune-boosting phenols.

## Pancakes

Preparation Time: 5 minutes
Cooking Time: 15 minutes
**Serves 1 grown-up and 1 little person**

### Ingredients

285ml full-fat milk
1 egg
1–2tbsp plain flour
1tsp unsalted butter

**TO SERVE:** Fruit Purée (page 36), Fruit Compote (page 35), raisins, sultanas, full-fat natural yoghurt, chopped blueberries, Banana Ice Cream (page 181)

## Method

1. Measure the milk into a measuring jug, add the egg and whisk with a fork
2. Put the flour in a bowl and make a well in the centre, add the milk slowly and whisk briskly until the mixture has a batter-like consistency; chill in the fridge until needed
3. Heat the butter in a frying pan and ensure the whole of the base is coated
4. Pour a large spoonful of batter into the pan and tilt the pan so the batter is swirled around the base
5. When the underside is cooked, flip over and cook the other side
6. Once cooked, tip onto a plate, add your filling and roll

*Leftovers*: Fill any leftover pancakes with some wilted spinach, cream cheese or cottage cheese, and a pinch of grated nutmeg and chill in the fridge until lunch or dinner time.

*Adult add-on*: For an American twist: try stacking the pancakes and drizzling maple syrup over the pile.

# Fruity Flapjack

Preparation Time: 5 minutes
Cooking Time: 25 minutes
**Serves 1 grown-up and 1 little person**

## Ingredients

2 bananas
1 peach or nectarine
Handful of strawberries
Handful of raisins or sultanas
100g porridge oats
Unsalted butter for greasing

## Method

1. Preheat the oven to 180C/160C fan/gas 4
2. Mix all the ingredients together in a food processor. You're after a sticky consistency so add more oats if needed
3. Spoon into a greased muffin tray or shape into patties on a greased baking tray and pop in the oven for around 25 minutes

---

*Leftovers*: These keep in the fridge for several days and make a lovely, non-messy, healthy snack.
*Health*: Oats help stimulate melatonin so may help encourage a good night's sleep for your baby.

# Carrot Cake

Preparation time: 10 minutes
Cooking time: 30 minutes
**Serves 4 grown-ups and 2 little people**

## Ingredients

100g unsalted butter
100g sultanas
Juice and zest of 2 sweet oranges/
    clementines/satsumas
150g self-raising flour
1tsp mixed spice
1tsp ginger
½tsp bicarbonate of soda
2 eggs
1–2 medium carrots (grated)
1 apple (grated)

## Method

1. Preheat the oven to 180/160C fan/gas 4
2. Put the orange juice/zest, sultanas and butter in the microwave for 1 minute
3. Line and grease a small cake tin
4. Tip the flour, bicarbonate of soda, carrot, apple, ginger and mixed spice into a mixing bowl
5. Add the eggs to the orange mix and stir into the dry ingredients
6. Tip into the cake tin and put in the oven for 25–30 minutes or until you can pierce with a skewer and remove it clean

# Ice Lollies

Preparation Time: 10 minutes
Freezing Time: 8–10 hours
**Serves 1 little person**

## Ingredients

Orange juice, apple juice, or pineapple juice

## Method

1.  Pour the juice into lolly moulds and freeze

---

*Tip*: If you don't have lolly moulds, pour the juice into ice cube trays and pop in a small plastic spoon to act as the handle. The spoons that come with baby medicines are an ideal size.

*Tip*: Lollies can be very messy, so they make an ideal snack to enjoy in the garden!

*Health*: The cooling effect on the gums makes ice lollies perfect for teething babies.

*Health*: Vomiting and diarrhoea often lead to dehydration so replacing fluids is essential, yet a drink of cold water often irritates the stomach causing babies to vomit again. Serve a plain water ice lolly, which will slow down the drinking and reduce the shock to the stomach.

*Health*: Try mixing prune juice with apple juice for a constipation-busting lolly.

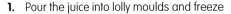

# Mango Sorbet

Preparation Time: 10 minutes
Freezing time: 6–8 hours
**Serves 1 grown-up and 1 little person**

## Ingredients

2 mangos
1 banana
Splash of apple juice

## Method

1. Pop all the ingredients in a food processor and blend
2. Pour into a freezer-proof container, cover and freeze for 6–8 hours or until ready to serve

---

*Tip*: Remove the sorbet from the freezer as you sit down for the main meal as it may take a while to defrost.

*Adult add-on*: Top with a dusting of icing sugar and a mint leaf for a dessert fit for a dinner party.

*Development*: Mangos have high levels of vitamin A, which promotes bone growth and tooth development.

*Health*: Mango contains vitamin A, which helps prevent dry skin.

*Health*: The coolness makes this lovely for little teethers.

# Apple Crumble

Preparation Time: 20 minutes
Cooking time: 40 minutes
**Serves 2 grown-ups and 2 little people**

## Ingredients

Leftover Apple Busters (page 184)
  or 6 eating apples (peeled, cored and chopped)
3tbsp plain flour
1tbsp oats
2 splashes of apple juice
1tsp unsalted butter

## Method

1. Preheat the oven to 180C/160C fan/gas 4
2. Melt the butter in a frying pan and add the apples with a splash of apple juice, stirring occasionally for around 10 minutes
3. Meanwhile, make the topping by whizzing the flour, butter and another splash of apple juice in a food processor (or mixing by hand); then stir in the oats
4. Spoon the apples into an ovenproof dish and cover with the oat topping
5. Pop in the oven for 40 minutes

*Tip*: Try combining the apples with blackberries or pear for an interesting twist.
*Tip*: Serve with Banana Custard (page 181) or Banana Ice Cream (page 181).
**Adult add-on**: Serve with custard, fresh cream or ice cream.

# Banana Ice Cream

Preparation Time: 5 minutes
Freezing time: 6–8 hours
**Serves 1 grown-up and 1 little person**

## Ingredients

3 mushy bananas

## Method

1. Mash the bananas, either by hand or in a food processor
2. Pop in a freezer-proof container and leave in the freezer overnight

> **Health**: If your baby is recovering from diarrhoea, bananas can be useful for replacing lost electrolytes.

# Banana Custard

Preparation Time: 5 minutes
**Serves 1 little person**

## Ingredients

2 mushy bananas
1tbsp full-fat natural yoghurt

## Method

1. Mash the bananas and yoghurt together, by hand or in a food processor, and serve

> **Tip**: A lovely, easy pudding served alone or as an accompaniment to Apple Crumble (page 180).
> **Leftovers**: Pop in the freezer overnight and serve for breakfast the next morning as a yummy yoghurt breakfast bar, dunked in Fruit Compote (page 35) or Fruit Purée (page 36).

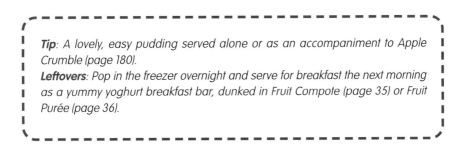

# Cheese Board

Preparation Time: 5 minutes
**Serves 2 grown-ups and 2 little people**

## Ingredients

A selection of pasteurised cheeses such as:
Yummy Yoghurt-Cheese (page 183), Baby Swiss,
  Cheddar, Edam, mozzarella, and cottage
Celery sticks
Seedless grapes (halved)
Oatcakes (page 202) or Oatcake Biscuits (page 203)

## Method

1. Serve chunks of cheese with the celery,
   grapes and Oatcakes or Oatcake Biscuits
   and allow your baby to gnaw on them

---

*Tip*: The National Diet and Nutrition Survey of Young people shows that 44% of boys and 50% of girls aged 4–18 still consume less than the recommended daily amount of calcium.

*Tip*: Avoid highly processed cheese, such as 'string cheese', soft spreads and 'dippers' as these are often high in salt.

*Adult add-on*: Serve with a selection of crackers and water biscuits.

*Development*: Cheese is a high source of calcium and phosphorous, which is ideal for rapidly developing bones and teeth.

*Health*: Organic milk, cheese and yoghurt may protect young children against eczema and asthma, researchers say. They found that infants raised on organic dairy products are a third less likely to suffer from allergies in the first two years of life than those fed non-organic dairy products.

# Yummy Yoghurt-Cheese

Preparation Time: 5 minutes
Chilling Time: 24 hours
**Serves 2 grown-ups and 2 little people**

## Ingredients

500ml full-fat natural yoghurt
2 coffee filters

## Method

1.  Line a sieve with the coffee filters,
    place over a bowl and pour in the yoghurt
2.  Pop in the fridge and leave for 24 hours
3.  You will find what remains in the sieve is
    a thick yoghurt-cheese ready for eating

---

*Tip*: Before straining, mix the yoghurt with a splash of fruit juice, Fruit Compote (page 35), or Fruit Purée (page 36) for a different flavour.
**Leftovers**: Try making Easy-Cheesy Pasta (page 92) with any leftovers or spread on Oatcakes (page 202) or Oatcake Biscuits (page 203) for a tasty snack.

# Apple Busters

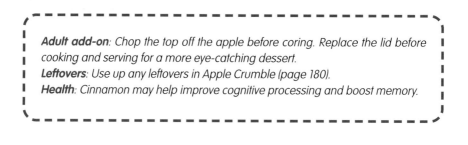

Preparation Time: 10 minutes
Cooking Time: 45 minutes
**Serves 1 grown-up and 1 little person**

## Ingredients

2 eating apples (sweet variety)
2tsp cinnamon
2 small handfuls of raisins,
   sultanas or other dried fruit

## Method

1. Preheat the oven to 180C/160C fan/gas 4
2. Wash and core the apples, placing on a piece of foil
3. Sprinkle with the cinnamon and fill the apples with the dried fruit
4. Wrap each apple individually in foil and bake in the oven for 45 minutes or until they feel squidgy
5. Once cooked, allow to cool, remove the skin and serve

---

*Adult add-on*: Chop the top off the apple before coring. Replace the lid before cooking and serving for a more eye-catching dessert.
*Leftovers*: Use up any leftovers in Apple Crumble (page 180).
*Health*: Cinnamon may help improve cognitive processing and boost memory.

# Fruit Jelly

Preparation Time: 15 minutes
Chilling Time: 2–4 hours
**Serves 2 grown-ups and 2 little people**

## Ingredients

3tbsp leftover Fruit Compote (page 35)
  or Fruit Purée (page 36)
1tbsp gelatine or agar flakes
300ml fruit juice
100ml water

**TO SERVE:** Banana Ice Cream (page 181);
  Banana Custard (page 181), or Baked Custard (page 187)

## Method

1. In a saucepan, heat the gelatine/agar and water until dissolved
2. Add the juice and continue to stir for 5 minutes
3. Pop in a jelly mould or bowl and cool for 5 minutes in the fridge. Before it sets, stir in the Fruit Purée or Fruit Compote and return to the fridge for several hours until fully set

# Banana Rice Pudding

Preparation Time: 5 minutes
Cooking Time: 5 minutes
**Serves 1 grown-up and 1 little person**

## Ingredients

100g cooked brown rice
140ml full-fat milk
Pinch of cinnamon
Pinch of nutmeg
1 banana (sliced)

**TO SERVE:** Fruit Purée (page 36) or Fruit Compote (page 35)

## Method

1. Put all ingredients in a food processor and blend until the desired consistency
2. Serve hot or cold

> *Tip*: Vary the consistency based on your baby's developmental stage. Younger babies may prefer a stodgier pudding to easily pick up with their fingers.
> *Health*: Bananas contain magnesium, which has a relaxing effect on muscles and may help your baby unwind and sleep after a busy day.

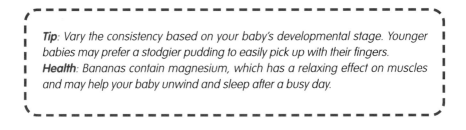

# Baked Custard

Preparation Time: 5 minutes
Cooking Time: 30 minutes
**Serves 1 grown-up and 1 little person**

## Ingredients

2 egg yolks (beaten)
240ml full-fat milk
1 mashed banana
Vanilla seeds from a pod (optional)

## Method

1. Preheat the oven to 180C/160C fan/gas 4
2. Spoon the mashed banana into the bottom of an ovenproof dish
3. Mix the milk, vanilla seeds (if using) and egg yolks together and pour over the banana
4. Make a bain-marie by placing the dish into another, larger, ovenproof dish and carefully pour in hot water. The water should come to about halfway up on the smaller dish
5. Bake for 30 minutes or until the custard is set. Carefully remove from the larger dish, and allow to cool before placing in the fridge

*Tip*: To prepare the vanilla pod, split lengthways using a paring knife and scrape the seeds from within. Store any leftover pods in an airtight container in a cupboard for up to two years.

*Tip*: When adding the hot water to the larger dish, it's easier to place the empty dish on your pulled-out oven rack, place the smaller dish inside, pour in the water, and then carefully slide the rack back into the oven. This saves walking to the oven with a heavy dish full of hot water.

*Adult add-on*: Add 1tsp vanilla extract to the mix for a more familiar custard taste. We don't recommend adding this to your child's dish due to the alcohol content.

*Leftovers*: Use the leftover egg whites to make a Frittata (page 85).

*Health*: Milk contains tryptophan, an amino acid, which acts as a sedative and may help your baby sleep.

*Health*: Vanilla can help calm a little one's upset tummy by reducing a fever and fighting the infection.

# Banana and Mango Smoothie

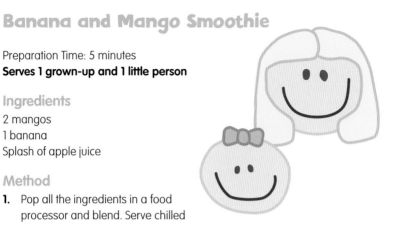

Preparation Time: 5 minutes
**Serves 1 grown-up and 1 little person**

## Ingredients

2 mangos
1 banana
Splash of apple juice

## Method

1. Pop all the ingredients in a food processor and blend. Serve chilled

---

*Leftovers*: Pour into lolly moulds and freeze. If you don't have lolly moulds, use an ice cube tray. Lean a plastic spoon (the ones used for medicines are ideal) in each cube and freeze. The spoon will act as a great handle for your lolly or, as it melts, they can spoon it out like ice cream.

**Adult add-on**: Pour the smoothie into a plastic bottle and freeze. Pop it in your bag in the morning and by lunchtime it will have defrosted into a yummy, healthy smoothie for lunch.

# Watercress, Melon and Pear Smoothie

Preparation Time: 10 minutes
**Serves 1 grown-up and 1 little person**

## Ingredients

1 galia melon (peeled and pips removed)
2 pears (peeled, pips and core removed)
Handful of watercress

## Method

1.  Pop all the ingredients in a food
    processor and blend. Serve chilled

*Jane's Tip*: I like to serve a smoothie to my older children after school in a plastic
glass with a cocktail umbrella. It's our own little 'cocktail hour'.

## Sleepy-Pud

Preparation Time: 10 minutes
**Serves 1 little person**

### Ingredients

40g oats
A few glugs of full-fat milk
1 banana (sliced)

### Method

1. Prepare the porridge on the stove or microwave following the instructions on the box
2. Mash in the banana, allow to cool and serve

*Leftovers*: Make banana-flavoured Porridge Pancakes (page 34).
*Health*: Oats, bananas and milk contain melatonin and amino acids, which encourage sleep.

# Cherry Quinoa

Preparation Time: 5 minutes
Cooking Time: 10 minutes
**Serves 1 little person**

## Ingredients

Handful of cherries (washed and stones removed)
40g quinoa
100ml apple juice
100ml water

## Method

1. Warm the cherries in the microwave for 30 seconds to soften
2. Cook the quinoa, water and apple juice in the microwave for 3 minutes
3. Remove, stir and continue to cook for a further 3–5 minutes or until the quinoa is cooked
4. Remove and stand for 2 minutes, drain any excess liquid and stir in the cherries

*Development*: Although not a common allergen, babies less than 8 months may find it hard to digest cherries so watch out for them in their nappies.
*Health*: Cherries are high in vitamin A, which may help ease the pain and inflammation from teething.

# Chapter Nine

# Snacks

As your child continues to grow he will naturally become more active. However, children's stomachs are still small and most are unable to eat enough food at one mealtime to keep them going until the next. Healthy snacks are therefore an important part of their diet. Not only do snacks help maintain your little one's energy levels, they also help keep his blood sugar levels stable, which may prevent hunger-induced tantrums.

Think about the time at which you are offering the snack; you probably don't want to offer him something just before you serve dinner as it may take the edge off his hunger, but offering snacks at regular times, such as one mid-morning and one mid-afternoon, means you're allowing your child the opportunity to identify when he is hungry or full. Be mindful of your child grazing constantly throughout the day as this can lead to bad eating habits and dental decay.

Each time your child eats, acidic chemicals are released into his mouth to start breaking down the food as he chews. These acids remain in the mouth for around twenty minutes following eating, forming an acid-bath for his little teeth. Continuous grazing throughout the day could therefore lead to dental decay due to the teeth being exposed to the acid for longer periods. There is no hard and fast rule for snacks but many families find two snacks per day (one in the morning and one in the afternoon) work well.

Processed foods laden with sugar, salt and additives such as sweets, crisps and chocolate offer very little nutrition, short bursts of energy and are bad for teeth so it is important that healthy snacks are offered. When deciding which snack to offer your child you may want to consider offering a food group he chose not to eat at his mealtime, for example, if he did not eat his salad at lunchtime you may want to offer some tomatoes and cucumber sticks as an afternoon snack. This will help ensure your child benefits from all the food groups throughout the day and means less stress for you at mealtimes if he chooses not to eat everything on offer.

On the next few pages are some yummy, sugar- and salt-free snacks suitable for the whole family.

# Wholemeal Bread Sticks (P/LB)

Preparation Time: 45 minutes
Cooking Time: 20 minutes
**Makes 12 regular bread sticks**

## Ingredients
450g wholemeal bread flour
1 (7g) sachet fast-action dried yeast
300ml tepid water
2tbsp olive oil

## Method
1. Dust a baking tray with some flour. Put the remaining flour and yeast into a bowl and add the water. Mix to make a soft, but not sticky, dough
2. Knead for 10 minutes on a lightly floured surface
3. Divide the mixture into 12 parts and roll into bread stick shapes. Put onto the baking tray
4. Drizzle some cling film with olive oil and place over the baking tray, oil side down, and set aside somewhere warm for 30 minutes as the bread sticks rise and double in size
5. Preheat the oven to 200C/180C fan/gas 6
6. Remove the cling film and put the tray in the oven for 20 minutes or until the bread sticks turn golden brown and are firm to touch

---

*Tip*: For mini Bread Sticks: at step 3, divide into 24 parts.
*Tip*: Freeze any leftover baked sticks in a freezer bag. They will defrost within an hour of removing from the freezer.
*Adult add-on*: Mini Bread Sticks make fun canapés with dips of Guacamole (page 140), taramasalata and hummus. Before baking, sprinkle with sea salt and fresh black pepper.
*Leftovers*: Use Bread Sticks as a 'dunker' in Natural Fruity Yoghurt (page 171) and Smoothies (pages 188–9) or serve with a Cheese Board (page 182).
*Kerene's Tip*: Milo loves helping to make Bread Sticks. We get our hands all mucky with the dough and his delight when they blow up in size is a pleasure to see.

---

## Banana Bread (P/LB)

Preparation Time: 5 minutes
Cooking Time: 40 minutes
**Serves 2 grown-ups and 2 little people**

### Ingredients

4tbsp self-raising flour
1 egg
2–3 mushy bananas
2 handfuls of raisins or sultanas
1tsp unsalted butter for greasing

**TO SERVE:** Fruit Purée (page 36),
Fruit Compote (page 35)

### Method

1. Preheat the oven to 180C/160C fan/gas 4
2. Put the flour in a mixing bowl, add the rest of the ingredients and squidge with your hands until mixed together, to create a gooey, sludgy texture
4. Grease the muffin tray or loaf tin with the butter and spoon in the mixture
5. Bake in the oven for 30–40 minutes or until golden-brown and risen

> *Tip*: Check the Banana Bread is cooked by sticking a cocktail stick or wooden skewer into the centre. If it comes out clean then it is cooked.
> *Health*: Bananas contain melatonin and serotonin, which may help your baby sleep.

# Gingerbread People (P/LB)

Preparation Time: 15 minutes
Cooking Time: 15 minutes
**Makes 10–12 Gingerbread People**

## Ingredients

150g self-raising flour
50g butter
1tsp fresh ginger (grated) or ½tsp ground ginger
Splash of apple juice

## Method

1. Preheat the oven to 180C/160C fan/gas 4
2. Using your hands, rub the flour, butter and ginger together until it resembles bread-crumbs
3. Add a few drops of apple juice to bring the ingredients together to make a firm dough
4. Roll out on a floured surface and use a pastry cutter to make shapes of your choice
5. Pop in the oven on a greased or lined baking tray for 15 minutes or until golden

---

**Tip**: To make the dough wetter add more juice, or add more flour to make it less sticky.

**Health**: Ginger has a calming effect on the intestines and may help relieve the symptoms of diarrhoea. Ginger is also great for improving circulation and helping to speed up the healing of a bruise.

## Hot Cross Buns

Preparation Time: 2 hours 35 minutes
Cooking Time: 25 minutes
**Makes 12–15 small buns**

### Ingredients
125ml full-fat milk
1tsp dried yeast
50ml honey
50g unsalted butter
1tsp cinnamon
½tsp nutmeg
2 eggs (beaten)
500g self-raising flour
Handful of raisins
1 egg white (lightly beaten)
Extra honey to glaze

**TO SERVE:** Fruit Purée (page 36), Fruit Compote (page 35)

## Method

1. In a measuring jug, add the yeast to the milk and microwave for around one minute until the yeast dissolves
2. Tip the milk into a mixing bowl and slowly stir in the honey, butter, cinnamon, nutmeg and egg
3. Add the flour, mix well until a dough forms, and then knead on a floured surface for about 5 minutes. Cover the bowl with cling film and leave somewhere warm for an hour until the dough has doubled in size
4. Knead the dough for another 5 minutes then add the raisins, making sure they are well dispersed throughout the dough
5. Shape into a ball, cover again and leave for another 30 minutes
6. Divide the dough into 12–15 balls and place on a greased or lined baking tray with enough space between them to allow them to expand
7. Make a deep cross in the top of each bun, cover and leave to rise again for another 30 minutes
8. Preheat the oven to 200C/180C fan/gas 6
9. Brush the buns with the egg white and bake them in the oven for 15 minutes
10. Remove them, drizzle with the honey glaze
11. Return the buns to the oven for about 5–10 minutes
12. Remove when browned and allow to cool before serving

*Tip*: Don't be put off by the length of preparation time. There's plenty of waiting around involved with this recipe but it's a great one to make with toddlers as they watch the dough expand each time.

*Tip*: Lovely served with Fruit Compote (page 35) as a snack or a pudding.

## Fruity Cereal Bars (P/LB)

Preparation Time: 10 minutes
Cooking Time: 20 minutes
**Makes 8–10 Fruity Cereal Bars**

### Ingredients
100g plain flour
100g oats
Handful of chopped dried fruit, such as:
  raisins, cranberries, apricots, sultanas, figs, prunes
300ml orange or apple juice

### Method
1. Preheat the oven to 180C/160C fan/gas 4
2. Put all the ingredients in a bowl and mix with your hands until they form a stiff dough
3. Roll out the dough and cut into bars
4. Place on a greased or lined baking sheet and cook for around 20 minutes, until dry and hard

*Health: The vitamin C in oranges may help with a stuffy nose or hay fever.*
*Health: Apricots and raisins are high fibre foods, which may help relieve the symptoms of constipation.*

# Oaty Fruity Biscuits (P/LB)

Preparation Time: 15 minutes
Cooking Time: 15 minutes
**Makes 8–10 Oaty Fruity Biscuits**

## Ingredients

Dried fruit, such as: apricots, prunes or figs
Splash of apple juice or orange juice
1tsp unsalted butter
Handful of oats

## Method

1. Preheat the oven to 200C/180C fan/gas 6
2. Purée the dried fruit with some apple or orange juice until it's mushy
3. Melt the butter over a medium heat. Add the oats and fruit and stir together
4. Remove from the heat, allow to cool, divide and mould into biscuit shapes of your choice
5. Pop the biscuits onto a greased or lined baking tray and bake in the oven for 15 minutes or until they begin to brown

*Tip*: These are ideal for breakfast or popping in your bag for a snack at work.
*Leftovers*: Use leftover Fruit Purée (page 36) or Fruit Compote (page 35) in place of the dried fruit and juice purée.
*Health*: Apple juice has a softening effect on stools. For an extra boost, substitute part of the apple or orange juice with prune juice for a constipation-relieving biscuit.
*Jenny's Tip*: The fig biscuits are delicious – daddy thinks they're better than chocolate digestives!

## Banana Biscuits (P/LB)

Preparation Time: 15 minutes
Cooking Time: 10 minutes
**Makes 8–10 biscuits**

### Ingredients

2 mushy bananas
50g plain flour
175g oats
2tsp ground nutmeg
1tsp bicarbonate of soda
100ml apple juice
Handful sultanas or raisins

### Method

1. Preheat the oven to 200C/180C fan/gas 6
2. Mix the bananas, flour, oats, nutmeg and bicarbonate of soda in a bowl
3. Add enough apple juice to thoroughly moisten the ingredients
4. Add the dried fruit and mix together to form a dough
5. Divide into 8–10 parts, shape into the biscuit shapes of your choice and place on a greased or lined baking sheet
6. Bake for around 10 minutes, until golden brown

# Sweet Potato Wedges

Preparation Time: 5 minutes
Cooking Time: 15–20 minutes
**Serves 1 grown-up and 1 little person**

## Ingredients

2 sweet potatoes (cut into wedges)
1tbsp fresh thyme leaves (chopped) or 1tsp dried thyme
1tbsp olive oil

## Method

1. Preheat the oven to 200C/180C fan/gas 6
2. Toss the wedges in the oil and chopped thyme
3. Roast in the oven for 15–20 minutes or until golden brown

*Tip*: Thyme is a very easy herb to grow in the garden.
*Tip*: Sweet potato contains vitamin A, which will help promote your baby's visual development.
*Tip*: Replace sweet potatoes with baking potatoes for a yummy alternative.
*Health*: The oils in thyme are a natural antiseptic often found in mouthwash and may help soothe throat infections.

## Oatcakes (P/LB)

Preparation Time: 10 minutes
Cooking Time: 10 minutes
**Makes 6–8 biscuits**

### Ingredients

100g oatmeal
100g plain flour
75ml full-fat milk
1 egg
1tsp unsalted butter

### Method

1. Whizz all the ingredients (apart from the butter) in a food processor
2. Melt the butter in a frying pan over a medium heat
3. Dollop biscuit-sized portions of the mixture into the pan and fry, turning until golden-brown on both sides

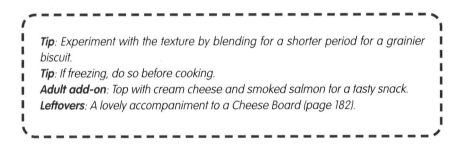

*Tip*: Experiment with the texture by blending for a shorter period for a grainier biscuit.
*Tip*: If freezing, do so before cooking.
**Adult add-on**: Top with cream cheese and smoked salmon for a tasty snack.
**Leftovers**: A lovely accompaniment to a Cheese Board (page 182).

# Oatcake Biscuits (P/LB)

Preparation Time: 10 minutes
Cooking Time: 30 minutes
**Makes 10–12 biscuits**

## Ingredients

250g oatmeal
Pinch of baking powder
1tbsp olive oil
Hot water

## Method

1. Preheat the oven to 180C/160C fan/gas 4
2. Mix the oatmeal and baking powder together in a bowl
3. Make a well in the middle of the ingredients and pour in the oil
4. Mix together to make a stiff paste, adding splashes of hot water as necessary
5. Shape into fat oatcakes and place on a greased baking tray in the oven for 20–30 minutes

> **Tip**: If freezing, do so before cooking.
> **Tip**: To prevent the biscuit curling up when baking, make the biscuits chunkier.
> **Leftover**: A lovely accompaniment to a Cheese Board (page 182).
> **Adult add-on**: Top with cream cheese and smoked salmon for a tasty snack.

## More Snack Ideas

Some other recipes in the book also work well as snacks. Why not try some of these:

| | | | |
|---|---|---|---|
| **Breakfast Bars** | Page 43 (P/LB) | **Fresh Seasonal Fruit** | Pages 44–5 (P/LB) |
| **Broccoli and** | | **Fruity Flapjack** | Page 176 (P/LB) |
| **Cheese Muffins** | Page 50 (P/LB) | **Hard Boiled Eggs** | Page 69 (P/LB) |
| **Crunchy Kale** | Page 68 (P/LB) | **Ice Lollies** | Page 178 (P/LB) |
| **Drop Scones** | Page 42 (P/LB) | **Natural Fruity** | |
| **Filo Fingers** | Page 59 (P/LB) | **Yoghurt (frozen)** | Page 171 (P/LB) |
| **Fruit sticks** | Page 31 (P/LB) | **Oaty Bars** | Page 48 (P/LB) |
| **French Toast** | Page 47 (P/LB) | **Veggie sticks** | Pages 29–31 (P/LB) |

Dried fruit such as apricots, raisins and sultanas all work well as a quick, healthy snack.

Chapter Ten

# Drinks

We all know we should drink at least eight glasses of water a day but what about our babies? For young children and babies drinking enough fluid is essential to health and well-being. A high proportion of a child's body weight is water so it's vital to keep young-sters properly hydrated. Read on to find out what your child should be drinking and when.

## Milk

Currently, the Department of Health recommends that babies should be exclusively milk-fed, by either breast or bottle, up until six months of age, after which solids can be introduced into the diet. In line with these guidelines, parents are advised that other fluids may be introduced at the same time although your baby's main drink will still be her milk; (500–600ml per day) whether formula or breast.

## Water

Dentists, health visitors and doctors all recommend that the best 'between meal' drink for a child is water and early introduction will encourage this good habit. But when it comes to water, is bottled your best option or should you opt for tap? The Drinking Water Inspectorate (DWI) insists that our tap water is safe and fresh, as well as being cheaper (and more eco-friendly) than bottled water. There are three different types of bottled water: natural mineral water (NMW), spring water and table water.

*Natural Mineral Water*: This comes from a ground water source, which is protected from all pollution and by law cannot be treated in any way. It undergoes two years of stringent analysis before it can be classed as an NMW. It is the purest form of water. However, NMWs contain high levels of minerals, some of which can be dangerous for your baby or toddler. For example, the calcium levels in some mineral waters can be too high for a baby's kidneys to cope with. Similarly, the sodium levels in many NMWs are much higher than the recommended 350mg a day for 1-year-old babies. Since December 2003, NMWs suitable for making up formula must be labelled as such.
*Spring Water*: Comes from a single non-polluted ground water source but unlike NMWs it can undergo some permitted treatments, although it must comply with Drinking Water Regulations. Unlike NMWs, there is no legislation requiring the mineral content to be printed on the bottle and because of this it's probably best avoided for your baby as there is no way of determining the sodium or mineral content.

*Table Water*: Is the trade name applied to other bottled drinking water. It applies to water that may come from more than one source and may include the public water supply. You should treat this water in the same way that you would treat normal tap water if using it to prepare feeds for your baby (i.e. boil and cool it). Ultimately, the choice is yours.

> **Note**: All water, whether bottled or tap should be boiled and cooled prior to making up infant formulas or giving as a drink to babies under six months.

## Fruit Juice

Because your little one may want to have a slurp from your cup, it's good for the family to start replacing carbonated, sugar-laden drinks with fruit drinks.

Avoid fruit squashes as these often contain artificial additives such as sweeteners and colourings. Instead, opt for those labelled High Juice, which often contain a higher fruit juice content.

Diluted fresh fruit juice can make a handy drink; fruit contains natural sugar, so dilute a splash of juice with water (about a 1:10 ratio).

Drinks with artificial sweeteners such as saccharin and aspartame should not be given to children under three years old. Research into the effects of sweeteners and their effect as carcinogens is still being conducted. We do not recommend offering these products to any child, as they provide no nutritional value.

The main problem with fruit juice is that it is filling and will decrease your child's appetite for other more nutritious foods. The British Nutrition Foundation recommends only serving juices at mealtimes, and only serving them in a cup.

> **Health**: Hard stools are often due to lack of fluid. Encourage a constipated child to drink more water. Combining water with apple or prune juice can have a laxative effect, so this should really get things moving.

## Cups

Now is a good time to start thinking about using a cup for your baby. The School of Dentistry at the University of Birmingham says, 'Encourage your baby to drink from a cup as soon as they can hold one and try to discourage bottle feeding by the age of one year.'

This is because most drinks, other than water, contain some form of sugar. Using a teat means there is prolonged contact with newly growing teeth, which increases the risk of tooth decay. The use of teats can also inhibit speech development.

The Doidy Cup is a great invention. The sloping nature means your little one (and you) can see when the liquid is reaching her mouth and so it is much easier to drink from than a normal cup. It can still be quite messy to begin with so be sure to pop a bib on.

> **Nicola's Tip**: Most fruit blitzed in a blender will make a healthy fruit drink. Just add a splash of water to dilute.

## Chapter Eleven

# Eating Out

## Essential Kit

Portable highchair or harness
Cool bag with all your food
Cup, spoons, forks
Baby wipes (for cleaning face and hands)
Antibacterial wipes (for cleaning table surfaces and highchair tables, etc.)
Plastic and cloth bibs

## Warming Food

One of the things you may notice when you venture out to eat with your child is how many eating establishments are unable to heat up food you have brought with you due to Health and Safety regulations (in case the child is scalded by hot food). However, these same places are often more than happy to offer you a bowl of hot water in which to heat your food. Go figure!

The bowl of boiling water may not be a suitable solution for two obvious reasons: a) a bowl of boiling hot water could be a danger to your child (especially for those little wrigglers) and b) it does nothing to heat the food whatsoever. If you do opt for the boiling water, choose a table where you can put the bowl out of harm's way.

Some child-friendly places kindly make a communal microwave available. Often these are well-used and food-splattered so rest a lid on top of the meal you're warming as who knows what delights are going to fall into your dish otherwise. Always check your food container is microwave-safe before using. Many plastics release carcinogens when heated, which may leech into the food so don't be afraid to ask staff for a separate bowl to heat your food in.

When reheating food, you need to ensure that it is piping hot throughout. Don't be tempted just to partially warm the food, so that your little one will be able to eat it immediately – it needs to be thoroughly heated in order to destroy any bacteria that may be present. You should then set it aside and allow to cool to a comfortable serving temperature.

Taking food that can be enjoyed cold is often a safer option when you're eating out at an unfamiliar place. Creating a picnic lunch for your child can be quite fun and colourful if it contains a variety of different foods with an array of flavours. Switching meals around can be another way of managing eating out. It is common for lunches to be cold and dinners to be hot so if you're eating out at dinner time, maybe offer the hot meal at lunch where you know you've got the ability to serve it hot.

*Jane's Tip*: I often microwave food before I go out so it's piping hot and pop it straight away into a thermos flask. By lunchtime it's cooled to the perfect temperature.

Eating out with your child can be challenging but also lots of fun. Children love to copy and parents often find their fussy eater eats better when dining with friends, as opposed to eating alone at home. It is often when eating out that parents are grateful for baby-led weaning. When the cool bag has been forgotten or a long car journey has caused an unscheduled stop, being able to order from a normal menu for your child will seem like a dream come true. Forget the inevitable children's menu of chicken nuggets, chips and beans (would you eat them?), order properly for yourself and offer some to your little one or order an extra half portion for them. From this book you know what your child should be eating and their likes and dislikes so be confident.

*Tip*: Food served in a restaurant often arrives far too hot for your little one to eat. It may be useful to have a selection of small toys, paper and crayons or books in your bag to keep them occupied whilst they are in the highchair waiting for their food to cool. If you have an active toddler on your hands, don't sit them in the high-chair too early otherwise they may quickly become restless.

## Picnics and Lunch Boxes

Enjoying family days out can often require you to prepare a picnic to take along. The following recipes and items may give you ideas as to what you could include to create colourful and tasty picnics. You may also get inspiration as to what to include in your child's school lunch box.

Hard Boiled Eggs (page 69)

Hummus or Guacamole (page 140) served
  with Bread Sticks (page 193), crackers or
  pitta bread

Sausage Rolls (page 161)

Broccoli and Cheese Muffins (page 50)

Sandwiches (page 52)

Pitta Pizza (page 54)

Chunks or cubes of cheese

Fruit or veggie slices or chunks

Dried fruit

Throughout the Lunch and Lighter Bites and Snacks chapters, there are additional recipes that are suitable served cold and are ideal for picnics or lunch boxes. Just look out for the (P/LB) symbol. Salads add beautiful colour to any picnic or lunch box, are versatile and are a great way of getting vegetables into your child's diet. Since the ingredients are often served raw, they are full of vitamins and minerals. Salads are great for encouraging your child to experience different textures and to hear how crunchy some foods sound when eaten raw. Simply chop and slice any vegetables you have in your fridge and pop them into a storage container, or you may like to try some of the recipes in this chapter, which are firm family favourites.

## Packing Food

Pack your food in a cool bag at an appropriate temperature for the food type. For example, yoghurt will need to be kept cold so adding an ice pack to your bag can be helpful. Keep warm foods in a thermos.

# Tricolour Salad

Preparation Time: 15 mins
**Serves 1 grown-up and 1 little person**

## Ingredients

1 ripe avocado (peeled and chopped)
2 large tomatoes (chopped)
Mozzarella (sliced or chopped)
Romaine lettuce

## Method

1. Chuck the chopped avocado, mozzarella and tomato into a bowl and mix
2. Lay some washed Romaine lettuce across the bottom of the plate/storage container and spoon the mixture over the leaves

## Crunchy Green Salad

Preparation Time: 15 minutes
**Serves 1 grown-up and 1 little person**

### Ingredients

Lettuce and/or spinach leaves (roughly torn)
8 slices of cucumber (chopped)
1 ripe avocado (chopped)
2 spring onions or a handful of chives
2 stalks of celery (chopped)
½ green apple (chopped)

### Method

1. Simply wash and chop the vegetables and mix in with the torn lettuce and/or spinach

*Tip*: Add a sprinkling of mustard cress if you have it.

## Egg Salad

Preparation Time: 15 minutes
Cooking Time: 8 minutes
**Serves 1 grown-up and 1 little person**

### Ingredients

Lettuce and/or spinach leaves
Rocket
3 Hard Boiled Eggs (page 69), cut into quarters
8 cherry tomatoes, halved
Sprinkling of mustard cress (optional)

### Method

1. Place the leaves into a bowl and toss in the eggs and tomatoes
2. Sprinkle with the cress, if using, and serve

# Rainbow Salad

Preparation Time: 15 minutes
**Serves 1 grown-up and 1 little person**

## Ingredients

Lettuce, spinach or rocket
8 slices of cucumber (halved)
8 cherry tomatoes (halved) or 2 large tomatoes (diced)
4 radishes (quartered)
2 beetroots (diced)
½ can of sweetcorn (drained)
½ orange pepper (diced)

## Method

1.  Mix all the ingredients together in a bowl and serve

# Potato Salad

Preparation Time: 10 minutes
Cooking Time: 30 minutes
**Serves 1 grown-up and 1 little person**

## Ingredients

500g new potatoes
Handful of chives (finely chopped)
2 stalks of celery (chopped)
4tbsp crème fraiche
½tsp lemon juice
Black pepper to season

## Method

1. Steam or boil the new potatoes for about 30 minutes until soft; set aside to cool
2. Tip all the remaining ingredients into a bowl and mix
3. Once the potatoes have cooled, halve and stir into the crème fraiche mix

*Tip*: *For some protein, add some sliced Hard Boiled Eggs (page 69) to the salad.* **Adult add-on**: *For something a little different, add some cooked, sliced bacon to the mix*

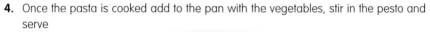

# Pesto Pasta Salad

Preparation Time: 10 minutes
Cooking Time: 15 minutes
**Serves 2 grown-ups and 1 little person**

## Ingredients

200g dried or fresh pasta
Glug of olive oil
4tsp Pesto (page 117)
2 cloves of garlic (chopped)
1 shallot (finely chopped)
6 mushrooms (quartered)
1 leek (finely chopped)
1 pepper (chopped)

> *Tip*: This salad is delicious served hot or cold.
> **Adult add-on**: Add a sprinkling of toasted pine nuts for extra flavour and crunch.

## Method

1. Cook the pasta as per the packet instructions
2. Heat the oil in a pan and cook the garlic, leek and shallot over a gentle heat
3. Add the mushrooms and pepper and cook for another couple of minutes
4. Once the pasta is cooked add to the pan with the vegetables, stir in the pesto and serve

# Penny's Salmon Quinoa

Preparation Time: 10 minutes
Cooking Time: 20 minutes
**Serves 2 grown-ups and 1 little person**

## Ingredients

150g quinoa
220ml Chicken Stock (page 116)
1 fillet of salmon or 1 small tin of red
  salmon
Juice of 1 lemon
Glug of olive oil
1 avocado (diced)

10 cherry tomatoes (quartered)
½ pepper (diced)
½ cucumber (cubed)
2 spring onions (finely chopped)
Handful of fresh parsley (chopped)
Handful of mint leaves (chopped)
Black pepper to season

## Method

1. Rinse the quinoa thoroughly and cook, as per the packet instructions, in the stock. Bring to the boil and simmer until all the liquid has been absorbed and the grains have separated
2. If using fresh salmon place the fillet under a preheated grill, on high, for 8 minutes (you may want to use the zest of the lemon and mix it with 1tsp of olive oil to brush onto the fillet before grilling)
3. Combine the lemon juice and olive oil and pour over the quinoa in a bowl, add the herbs and the vegetables and stir
4. Once the salmon fillet is cooked, flake the flesh (or add the tinned salmon) and mix it into the quinoa salad; season to taste

*Tip*: For the last 5–10 minutes of cooking time for the quinoa, place a lid on the saucepan to keep the quinoa moist.

# Couscous Salad

Preparation Time: 10 minutes
Cooking Time: 15 minutes
**Serves 1 grown-up and 1 little person**

## Ingredients

250g couscous
Glug of olive oil
300ml boiling water or Chicken Stock (page 116)
½ courgette (chopped)
½ aubergine (chopped)
1 pepper (chopped)
2 shallots (finely chopped)
2 cloves of garlic (crushed)

## Method

1. Heat some oil in a frying pan and gently cook the shallots and garlic
2. Add the aubergine, courgette and pepper and cook until softened
3. Place the couscous into a bowl with the water or stock, stir thoroughly, cover and leave to stand for 10 minutes, then separate the grains with a fork
4. Add the cooked vegetables to the couscous, mix thoroughly and serve

## Chapter Twelve

# Hints and Tips

## Oven Temperature Guide

|  | Electric °C | Electric °C (fan) | Gas Mark |
|---|---|---|---|
| Very cool | 110 | 90 | ¼ |
|  | 120 | 100 | ½ |
| Cool | 140 | 120 | 1 |
|  | 150 | 130 | 2 |
| Moderate | 160 | 140 | 3 |
|  | 180 | 160 | 4 |
| Moderately Hot | 190 | 170 | 5 |
|  | 200 | 180 | 6 |
| Hot | 220 | 200 | 7 |
|  | 230 | 210 | 8 |
| Very Hot | 240 | 220 | 9 |

## Spoon Measures

| Metric | Imperial |
|---|---|
| ¼tsp | 1.25ml |
| ½tsp | 2.5ml |
| ¾tsp | 3.75ml |
| 1tsp | 5ml |
| 1tbsp | 15ml |

## Wet Measures

| Metric | Imperial |
|--------|----------|
| 30ml | 1fl oz |
| 60ml | 2fl oz |
| 90ml | 3fl oz |
| 120ml | 4fl oz |
| 150ml | 5fl oz/¼ pint |
| 180ml | 6fl oz |
| 210ml | 7fl oz |
| 240ml | 8fl oz |
| 270ml | 10fl oz |
| 300ml | 11fl oz |
| 450ml | 16fl oz |
| 600ml | 21fl oz |

| Metric | Imperial |
|--------|----------|
| 140ml | ¼ pint |
| 285ml | ½ pint |
| 425ml | ¾ pint |
| 570ml | 1 pint |
| 850ml | 1½ pints |
| 1.14l | 2 pints |
| 1.42l | 2½ pints |

## Dry Measures

| Metric | Imperial |
|--------|----------|
| 7g | ¼oz |
| 15g | ½oz |
| 25g | 1oz |
| 50g | 2oz |
| 75g | 3oz |
| 100g | 4oz |
| 150g | 5oz |
| 175g | 6oz |
| 200g | 7oz |
| 225g | 8oz |
| 250g | 9oz |
| 275g | 10oz |
| 325g | 11oz |
| 350g | 12oz |
| 375g | 13oz |
| 400g | 14oz |
| 425g | 15oz |
| 450g | 16oz/1lb |

For ease of use, gram/millilitre conversions have been rounded to the nearest ounce/fluid ounce, and pint conversions are correct to the nearest five millilitres.

## The Pantry

**Eggs**: An essential ingredient for making quick meals, whether Scrambled Eggs (page 40) on Toast (page 38) for breakfast, an Omelette Crêpe (page 51) for lunch or Drop Scones (page 42) for dessert. Try to buy at least free-range, if not organic, and use when fresh.

**Bread**: A loaf in the freezer means if you've nothing else you can always make some Toast (page 38) for breakfast, and a Sandwich (page 52) for lunch, by which time hopefully you will have popped to the shops to get something for dinner.

**Unsalted butter**: Most brands have a salt-free variety and it's useful for frying through to spreading on bread.

**Stock cubes**: Salt-free or low-salt stock cubes are available in most supermarkets or health food shops. Always have vegetable, beef and chicken cubes in your cupboard.

**Plain flour, self-raising flour**: Useful for thickening a sauce and baking cakes.

**Tinned chopped tomatoes**: Always have plenty of these in your cupboards.

**Tomato purée**: Check the packaging, as many are low in salt or salt-free.

**Wine**: Some of the *adult add-on* suggestions recommend wine. With cooking, the alcohol is burned off and leaves harmless residues, which enhance the flavour.

**Lentils**: There are lots of different types of lentils such as split, green and puy. Whichever you choose, check to see if they need pre-cooking before embarking on a recipe

**Dried pasta and rice**: Boiling some pasta or rice and mixing in some tinned tomatoes will always make a quick dinner. Experiment with different types and shapes.

**Tinned fish**: Tuna or sardines can be used as sandwich fillings, stirred into pasta or simply served with some vegetables for a quick dinner.

**Cheese**: Whether it's to serve in sandwiches, to melt on vegetables or to serve as chunks, cheese is a versatile ingredient essential to all fridges.

## Defrosting Frozen Food

Most of us who endured Home Economics classes at secondary school will remember that you can't refreeze previously frozen foods. This is true when they're refrozen in their same state, for example, defrosting a steak, not cooking it and re-freezing. This is not recommended. However, it is safe to defrost an uncooked ingredient (some of your meals may use frozen ingredients such as chicken or beef mince), cook it to create dishes such as Meaty Bolognese (page 125) or Chicken and Apple Sausages (page 58) and freeze the cooked dish. These are safe to be thawed, reheated and served – but not frozen again! The only exception would be if the meal contained breast milk, as it is not safe to re-freeze previously frozen breast milk.

To ensure food is safe to eat after freezing, follow these guidelines:

- Defrost food slowly in a fridge or cool place. Never leave to defrost in a warm place as this is the perfect breeding ground for harmful bacteria to grow.
- Whilst defrosting, cover the food loosely. This might mean resting a lid on top of a container, rather than leaving it sealed.
- After it has defrosted thoroughly, cook the food as soon as possible.

## Storing Frozen Food

When freezing food be sure to label with a date, as different foods can be stored for different lengths of time in the freezer.

Prepared meals . . . . . . . . . . . . . 4–6 months
Bread . . . . . . . . . . . . . . . . . . . . . . 2–3 months
Fruit and vegetable purée . . . . 6–8 months
Fish portions . . . . . . . . . . . . . . . 3–4 months
Chicken . . . . . . . . . . . . . . . . . . . . 4–6 months
Minced beef . . . . . . . . . . . . . . . . 3–4 months

## Cooking and Kitchen Equipment

Make your life a little easier by investing in some kitchen equipment. Nothing on this list is essential; they are simply some gadgets we've found handy:

**Steamer**: Steaming vegetables can help retain more nutrients than boiling. There's also no chance of the pan boiling over whilst you do an emergency nappy change.

**Bread maker**: Most bread on sale today contains salt and preservatives to prolong the freshness. A bread maker is an ideal investment to make Wholemeal Salt-Free Bread (page 39), Wholemeal Bread Sticks (page 193) and Pizza Bases (page 122). Many models allow you to add the ingredients, set the timer and wake up to the wonderful aroma of freshly baked bread. Yummy!

**Food processor**: A handy gadget. It can dice an onion, blend a soup or whisk up a cake mixture in a few seconds. We are fond of the Kenwood Mini-Chopper, which creates less washing up. For greater volumes shop around for a larger model.

**Food containers**: Invest in child-friendly BPA-free plastic food containers for leftovers and transporting food.

**Freezer bags**: Good for storing larger portions for family meals, and individual foods, such as Chicken Fingers (page 62), Broccoli and Cheese Muffins (page 50) and Wholemeal Bread Sticks (page 193) etc.

**Purée/ice cube trays**: There are plenty of trays on the market designed to take individual purée portions, and ice cube trays work just as well.

**Chopping knife**: Have a single, good quality knife, which you are comfortable using. We find the Global 14cm Vegetable Chopper a really versatile knife.

**Paring knife**: A cheap paring knife can be handy for taking the tops off strawberries and quickly cutting a tomato in half.

**Vegetable peeler**: You'll probably buy a couple of these before you find the one that you like.

**Non-stick frying pan**: Invest in a large, non-stick frying pan that resembles a wok. They are great for one-pot dishes.

**Chopping boards**: We suggest having at least four chopping boards in different colours, for raw meat, raw fish, veggies/fruit and onions. Having a separate one for cooked meat might also be handy.

# Recipes by Cooking Time

As this book has been written by parents for parents we understand how life can be hectic. To help you manage your time we have listed the lunches and dinners according to the total time the dishes take to cook and prepare:

## Lunch/Lighter Bites/Picnic

**Under 15 minutes:**
Sandwiches (page 52)
Toasted Cheesy Pitta Pockets (page 53)
Chicken Liver Pâté (page 63)
Watercress and Spinach Pâté (page 64)
Crunchy Kale (page 68)
Tricolour Salad (page 209)
Crunchy Green Salad (page 210)
Rainbow Salad (page 211)
Hard Boiled Eggs (page 69)

**Under 30 minutes:**
Egg Salad (page 210)
Omelette Crêpes (page 51)
Turkey Burgers (page 56)
Turkey Meatloaf (page 57)
Chicken and Apple Sausages (page 58)
Filo Fingers (page 59)
Cheese Pastry Bites (page 60)
Chicken Fingers (page 62)
Pea and Mint Soup (page 65)
Kale Omelette (page 67)
Falafels (page 72)
Pesto Pasta Salad (page 213)
Penny's Salmon Quinoa (page 214)
Couscous Salad (page 215)

**Under 45 minutes:**
Broccoli and Cheese Muffins (page 50)
Fish Fingers (page 55)
Cheese and Tomato Tartlet (page 61)
Pitta Pizza (page 54)
Shortcrust Pastry (page 71)
Leek and Potato Soup (page 66)
Potato Salad (page 212)

**Over an hour:**
Quinoa and Kale Crustless Quiche (page 70)

## Dinner

**Under 15 minutes:**
Garlic Bread (page 120)
Onion Bhajis (page 141)
Welsh Rarebit (page 163)
Pizza Base (page 122)

**Under 30 minutes:**
Pizza Bolognese (page 77)
Pasty Bolognese (page 78)
Frittata (page 85)
Cauliflower and/or Broccoli Cheese (page 88)

Easy-Cheesy Pasta (page 92)
Arancini di Riso (page 84)
Pasta Gratin (page 101)
Pork Chops (page 102)
Tuna Rice (page 98)
Gnocchi (page 126)
Eggy Dumplings (page 103)
Bean Burgers (page 132)
Lamb Samosas (page 142)
Lamb Kofta (page 143)
Sammy's Saag Aloo (Vegetable Curry)
   (page 150)
Special Fried Rice (page 153)
Potato Curry (page 151)
Chicken and Sweetcorn Soup (page 158)
Scotch Eggs (page 160)
Lamb Kebabs (page 109)

**Under 45 minutes:**
Spicy Baked Chicken with Couscous
   (page 104)
Tricolore Pasta (page 96)
Chicken or Turkey and Broccoli Pasta
   (page 97)
Tuna Pasta Bake (page 99)
Beany Balls in Tomato Sauce (page 103)
Chicken Skewers (page 105)
Baked Veggie Pasta (page 106)
Turkey Meatball Casserole (page 108)
Chicken and Tomato Bake (page 113)
Puff Pastry Pizza (page 123)
Lemon Chicken Stir Fry (page 156)
Lamb Couscous Salad (page 110)
Fajitas (page 137)

**Under 1 hour:**
Chilli Bolognese (page 76)
Seafood Risotto (page 83)
Chicken or Turkey Mornay (page 90)
Lamb or Beef Rissoles (page 112)
Chicken Pancakes (page 114)
Spaghetti Carbonara (page 130)
Bean Chilli (page 136)
Mum's Chicken Curry (page 144)
Chicken Curry (Spice-Rack Slammer)
   (page 148)
Sausage Rolls (page 161)
Fish and Chips (page 166)
Vegetable Ratatouille (page 182)
Salmon and Broccoli Pasta Bake
   (page 89)
Chicken Kievs (page 107)

**Over 1 hour:**
Fish Pie (page 75)
Lentil Bolognese (page 124)
Meaty Bolognese (page 125)
Moroccan Stew (page 80)
Vegetarian Moussaka (page 79)
Cottage Pie (page 86)
Slow Roast Beef Brisket (page 164)
Lamb Stew (page 93)
Meat Balls (page 94)
Turkey Tagine (page 100)
Mama's Lasagne (page 121)
Chicken Cacciatore (page 128)
Chilli Con Carne (page 134)
Sweet and Sour Chicken/Prawn
   (page 152)
Fish Cakes (page 154)
Mini Meaty Pasties (page 162)
Lamb Roast Dinner (page 165)
Toad In The Hole With Onion Gravy
   (page 168)
Chicken Biryani (page 147)

# Further Information

If you have enjoyed this book and would like to know more about weaning and feeding your family, have a look at our website: www.yummydiscoveries.com

The School Food Trust (www.schoolfoodtrust.org.uk) and the Food Standards Agency (www.food.gov.uk) both have information about healthy eating. For further information on the Department of Health guidelines we have referenced, please visit www.dh.gov.uk

# Index